START YOUR OWN

TRAVEL HOSTING BUSINESS

Additional titles in **Entrepreneur's Startup Series**

Start Your Own

Entrepreneur.
MAGAZINE'S

 **STARTUP**

START YOUR OWN

TRAVEL
HOSTING
BUSINESS

AIRBNB · VRBO · HOMEAWAY
AND MORE

The Staff of Entrepreneur Media, Inc. & Jason R. Rich

Entrepreneur
PRESS®

Entrepreneur Press, Publisher
Cover Design: Andrew Welyczko
Production and Composition: Eliot House Productions

This publication is designed to provide accurate and authoritative information in regard to the subject matter covered. It is sold with the understanding that the publisher is not engaged in rendering legal, accounting or other professional services. If legal advice or other expert assistance is required, the services of a competent professional person should be sought.

Library of Congress Cataloging-in-Publication Data
Names: Rich, Jason, editor. | Entrepreneur Media, Inc., editor.
Title: Start your own travel hosting business: Airbnb, VRBO, Homeaway, and more/by the staff of
    Entrepreneur Media, Inc. and Jason Rich.
Other titles: Entrepreneur (Santa Monica, Calif.)
Description: Irvine, California : Entrepreneur Media, Inc., [2017] | Includes bibliographical references.
Identifiers: LCCN 2016055144 (print) | LCCN 2016057318 (ebook) | ISBN 978-1-59918-610-8
    (alk. paper) | ISBN 1-59918-610-1 (alk. paper) | ISBN 978-1-61308-366-6
Subjects: LCSH: Hotel management—Vocational guidance. | Bed and breakfast accommodations—
    Vocational guidance. | Entrepreneurship—Vocational guidance. | New business enterprises—
    Management.
Classification: LCC TX911.3.M27 S6987 2017 (print) | LCC TX911.3.M27 (ebook) | DDC
    647.94068—dc23
LC record available at https://lccn.loc.gov/2016055144

Printed in the United States of America

21 20 19 18 17   10 9 8 7 6 5 4 3 2 1

Contents

Acknowledgments

Thank you to Ronald Young and Jennifer Dorsey for once again inviting me to contribute to the Entrepreneur Press lineup of informative, small-business books. My gratitude also goes out to Karen Billipp and the team at Eliot House Productions for their work on this book. I'd also like to thank all of the Airbnb hosts and short-term rental experts who agreed to be interviewed and featured within this book.

Preface

Do you have a home or apartment with one or more extra bedrooms, or an entire property that you could offer as a short-term rental in order to earn extra income? Listing your property on a short-term rental service such as Airbnb allows people like you to become a travel host. If this type of part-time, money-making business opportunity seems appealing, or you want to learn more about it, *Start Your Own Travel Hosting Business* is the compressive, independent, unbiased, and informative how-to resource you need to read!

An ever-growing number of travelers from around the world have begun looking for lower-cost and more convenient accommodation alternatives, as opposed to staying at a traditional hotel or motel during their vacation, leisure, and/or business trips. As a result, online-based services, like Airbnb, FlipKey, HomeAway, Roomorama, and VRBO (Vacation Rental by Owner), have become extremely popular in recent years.

These services allow travel hosts (people like you), from all walks of life, to list their extra bedroom(s), or their entire home, condo, or apartment, as a short-term rental option for travelers. The popular short-term rental services help to quickly, securely, and conveniently match up travelers with hosts and handle many of the related financial transactions and reservation management responsibilities.

Depending on your geographic location and local laws and ordinances, what type of property you have to offer, the level of commitment you want to make as a host, and a variety of other factors, there are a variety of things to consider prior to becoming a travel host and choosing which short-term rental services to utilize.

First and foremost, *Start Your Own Travel Hosting Business* will help you make intelligent decisions, take appropriate actions and precautions, and deal with realistic expectations, while protecting yourself, your property, and your personal belongings as much as possible, once you become a host. It will help you quickly acquire the core knowledge you need to become a successful travel host and help you maximize your revenue, while avoiding the

► Consider Participating in an Airbnb Open Event

All of the interviews featured throughout this book have been added to provide you with an opportunity to learn from the firsthand experiences of other successful Airbnb hosts and short-term rental experts.

However, if you're serious about becoming an Airbnb host and want to focus more on making this a viable part-time or full-time revenue-generating opportunity, consider attending an Airbnb Open event.

Throughout the year, Airbnb hosts Airbnb Open events for their hosts. These are multiday social gatherings/professional networking conferences that allow you to freely interact with and learn from other hosts; attend interactive panel discussions; and listen to lectures from experts, Airbnb executives, and guest speakers.

For each event, pre-registration is required, and an attendance fee applies. To discover more about upcoming Airbnb Open events, including when and where they're scheduled to be held in the future, visit https://airbnbopen.com.

most common pitfalls and mistakes that are often made by first-time hosts. You'll also discover a variety of optional tools and resources at your disposal that will make handling your responsibilities as a travel host easier and less time consuming, while helping you increase your revenue and dramatically improve your chances for success.

In addition to providing detailed "how-to" and "step-by-step" information related to becoming a successful host with Airbnb (or a similar service), this book offers more than a dozen in-depth and exclusive interviews with a handful of veteran Airbnb hosts, as well as other executives within the short-term renting industry.

These hosts and experts each share their firsthand experiences and advice. From these interviews, you'll discover what works, what pitfalls to avoid, and how to make the most out of your hosting experience from a personal and financial standpoint. You'll also gain valuable insight about how to interact with your guests, earn the best possible ratings and reviews, and, at the same time, avoid common mistakes made by new hosts.

The primary focus of this book is on utilizing Airbnb as a travel host. However, much of the information you'll discover applies when working with any short-term rental service. If you have an appropriate property to offer, and you're interested in becoming a travel host, as you're about to discover, there's never been a better time to get started!

1

Changing the Way People Travel

D o you have a clean and comfortable spare room in your apartment or home where your friends and family enjoy staying when they visit? Perhaps you have a second apartment or vacation home that you don't use as often as you'd like, so it sits vacant for much of the year. Well, without making any long-term commitments, thanks to online-based hosting services, it's possible to share extra living spaces with other people, on a short-term basis, and generate some extra income in the process.

The main focus of this book is to teach you the ins and outs of being a successful Airbnb host (the most popular service of its type, by far) so that you're able to avoid the pitfalls, generate the highest revenue possible, and earn the best possible reviews and ratings from your guests.

In addition to Airbnb, however, there are a handful of other services (also online) that offer similar functionality and serve as a tool for matching up hosts with travelers. Some of these services are more specialized than Airbnb and cater to a specific clientele, or work only with hosts that offer a specific type of accommodation (see "Hosting Options Beyond Airbnb" on page 12).

While this book will introduce you to some of these other services, consider investing some time in your own research to determine, based on your own preferences and what you're offering, which service (in addition to or instead of Airbnb) will offer the best opportunity for you as a host. At first glance, the concept behind Airbnb and similar services is rather straightforward and simple. You provide guests with a place to stay, and they pay a nightly fee. However, before you opt to become a host, there are a handful of important factors you'll need to consider, misconceptions you'll need to overcome, preparations you'll need to make, and expenses you'll need to factor into your budget. There are also local and state laws you'll need to abide by, insurance to acquire, and additional planning to do.

It's important to understand, right from the start, that becoming an Airbnb host (or a host with a similar service) is not a get-rich-quick scheme, nor is it a viable money-making opportunity for everyone. Many factors, which you'll learn about shortly, go into whether you'll be able to consistently generate enough revenue as a host to make this opportunity worthwhile. However, if you make all the right moves, as a property owner, you can be successful. For example, out of the more than two million Airbnb hosts worldwide, some are making consistent money, continue to meet awesome new people, and absolutely love the opportunities that Airbnb provides.

According to research conducted by HomeAway (www.homeaway.com; see page 12) and its VacationRentals (www.vacationrentals.com) subsidiary, ". . . in 2016, nearly three-quarters (70 percent) of vacation rental owners are able to cover more than half of their mortgage through renting, and more than half (54 percent) cover three-quarters or more of their mortgage."

This research also showed that, "Vacation rental income comprises about a quarter (24 percent) of the average owner's income, from investing just fewer than 10 hours per week in the management and marketing of their vacation rental.

"From that relatively small amount of time spent advertising, fielding traveler inquiries, and coordinating the cleaning and maintenance of their property, owners use the money to pay off the mortgage (38 percent), upgrade and renovate the property (70 percent), fund their everyday living expenses (23 percent), and save for retirement (11 percent)."

Just be aware that there are many other hosts who have had to deal with a wide range of problems and frustrations, such as inconsiderate guests, unexpected fines, and, in some cases, fraud or crime and financial losses.

Discover Airbnb and What So Many Travelers Are Raving About

Founded in August 2008, Airbnb (www.airbnb.com) has evolved into a massive online community and marketplace that allows travelers from all walks of life to discover, book, and pay for short-term, nightly accommodations almost anywhere in the world. The Airbnb experience starts online, by visiting the Airbnb website or utilizing the official Airbnb mobile app on any smartphone or tablet that has internet access.

▶ Types of Accommodations That Can Be Offered on Airbnb

Airbnb allows hosts to offer a private guestroom or shared room (within a home, condo, or apartment, for example), an entire apartment, or an entire home (or condo living space) to guests. Accommodations should include a private or shared bathroom, as well as other amenities and options, such as use of a kitchen, in-home wifi, laundry facilities, and private or nearby parking.

When a private or shared guestroom is offered, this typically means that the property's host is living onsite. Based on space available, additional Airbnb guests may also be sharing the property.

When a traveler books an entire apartment or home, this means he is reserving the entire place for himself (and his travel companions). The host will initially greet him and be available during the guest's stay, but not living/staying on the actual premises.

Airbnb also offers unique or unusual places for travelers to stay, including historic castles, lakefront cottages, ski chalets, or even treehouses (that can be lived in). Other services that are similar to Airbnb (some of which you'll learn about later in this book) also offer yachts, family-friendly homes, or other types of unique accommodations.

Instead of offering traditional, full-service hotel rooms, bed-and-breakfast accommodations, timeshare opportunities, or resorts accommodations, for example, the entire focus of Airbnb is to provide travelers with a fast, easy, and low-cost way to stay in someone's guestroom, apartment, entire home, or even a castle.

Currently when travelers visit Airbnb they'll discover in excess of two million different places to stay, offered by Airbnb hosts in more than 34,000 cities (within more than 191 countries) around the world.

The vast majority of people who become Airbnb hosts are not full-time hospitality professionals. Instead, they're ordinary people, from all walks of life, with a vast assortment of backgrounds, who want to invite travelers to stay with them as a way to earn some extra income and meet new people.

For travelers, Airbnb is attractive for several reasons, including:

- ► Accommodations offer a less commercial, homier alternative to chain hotels and traditional accommodations.
- ► The nightly cost to stay at an Airbnb property is typically much less than a traditional hotel in that same area. As you'll discover, nightly pricing offered on Airbnb is based on a handful of criteria, but it is set by the host.
- ► Finding and booking a reservation is all done online, via the Airbnb.com website or mobile app.
- ► Travelers can quickly learn about a place to stay by reading its description, viewing the provided property photos, reading the host's profile, and reviewing the ratings and reviews that property and host have received from past Airbnb guests.
- ► Travelers can get their questions answered and their concerns addressed before making and prepaying for their reservation by contacting a prospective host via the Airbnb website or mobile app.

For Airbnb hosts, this service is attractive for several reasons, including:

- ► Hosts determine exactly what they're offering in terms of accommodations.
- ► Using the scheduling tool built into the Airbnb service, hosts can determine on what dates they want to make their property available. Airbnb

warning ⚠

Local laws, or apartment/condo/homeowner's association bylaws, often have their own rules and regulations pertaining to tenants and property owners who want to use their home, condo, or apartment to host paid guests via a service such as Airbnb. Failure to adhere to these laws/regulations could lead to hefty fines or eviction.

does not set a minimum or maximum number of nights per month or year that the property needs to be available.

▶ Hosts can communicate with and approve a guest before the reservation is made, unless the host turns on Airbnb's Instant Book feature. (New hosts should definitely keep this featured turned off, for reasons that will be explained in Chapter 2.)

▶ Hosts set their own nightly pricing. (Airbnb charges hosts a 3 percent host service fee on each reservation, which is how the service makes its money.)

▶ Hosts have the opportunity to meet, interact with, and, in some cases, socialize with their guests and make new friends.

▶ Airbnb (and services like it) offers a way to generate extra revenue, requiring a relatively small time commitment.

▶ The Airbnb service generates guest referrals, handles all of the reservation processing, and manages all of the financial transactions between the travelers and hosts.

Ten Important Factors to Consider Before Becoming a Host

Just as with any business opportunity, there are a handful of prerequisites that will help lead to your success as an Airbnb host.

Each of the following factors and considerations will be explained in much greater detail later within this book. However, as you first begin contemplating whether or not to become an Airbnb host, it's important to have a clear understanding of what you're signing up for.

The following are ten important factors to consider *before* you register to become an Airbnb host and begin having guests stay in your home or property.

1. Determine if local laws and/or the bylaws of your apartment complex, coop board, or homeowner's association prevent you from utilizing your home or apartment to host paid guests.
2. Determine if you have the personality, time, wherewithal, and willingness to interact with and manage guests (strangers) who will be staying in your home or property.
3. You're able to consistently provide a clean, comfortable, well-located, and desirable place for people to stay.
4. Your lifestyle and schedule allow you to be available to your guests and have people staying in your home. If you have young children or unfriendly pets, for example, this could be problematic.

5. You're willing to set competitive nightly pricing, based on what you're offering, competition, and demand in your geographic area.

6. You understand that as a host, customer service is one important key to your success. This will require an ongoing time commitment and effort on your part. Successful Airbnb hosts consistently receive positive feedback and great reviews from their guests. Earning anything less than stellar reviews and ratings will have a lasting and negative impact on your future success as a host.

7. Prior to actually having guests pay to stay with you, it's necessary to sign up to become a host with Airbnb (and/or a similar service). This requires you to create a detailed, accurate, and well-written profile that conveys information about yourself and what you're offering. You'll also need to take and share professional-quality photos of your property.

8. Before each guest checks in, it is necessary to prepare your property. This means both cleaning it and providing a selection of amenities that will make guests feel more comfortable and welcome.

9. Protect your own property and belongings. In addition to having adequate insurance (that covers you having paying guests stay in your home), make sure that any expensive décor (antiques, art, etc.), home electronics, and furnishings will remain safe, even with guests staying in your home.

10. Develop a comprehensive list of "house rules" that your guests will need to abide by. These rules needs to be spelled out and clearly communicated to guests, and then enforced, but also be fair. The rules you set will help determine the types of guests who stay with you. For example, as the host, your house rules can include: no smoking, no pets, no kids, no parties, no noise after 11:00 P.M., and/or no utilizing or accessing certain areas of your home or property. Guidelines for setting house rules are offered within Chapter 5, "Responding to Broken Rules."

After considering each of these factors, if you still believe you have what it takes to be a successful Airbnb host, and you have a guestroom, apartment, home, or an unusual place for guests to stay, then you may have stumbled upon an opportunity that will allow you to earn extra revenue. Being a travel host will also allow you to meet new people and better utilize your property in a way that offsets your property-related costs/expenses.

Here's a Quick Reality Check

Chances are, you're not the first potential host to learn about this opportunity in your geographic area. Based on where you live, and what you're offering in terms of guest accommodations, you may have intense competition from local hotels, motels, B&Bs, resorts, timeshare properties, and other Airbnb hosts.

If you set your nightly pricing too high based on what you're offering, potential guests will simply seek out alternate accommodations. However, if you set competitive nightly pricing that's much lower than your competition, you may determine that being a host is not financially rewarding after all. Setting the most desirable nightly price for your potential guests based on what you're offering and your location, as well as other factors, will be a key factor in your financial success as a host. This topic is covered in much greater detail within Chapter 4 "Preparing Your Property."

As you'll soon discover, the most successful Airbnb hosts offer:

▶ Affordable, clean, safe, and comfortable accommodations that cost less than the competition (local hotels, for example), at a fair price.

▶ Accommodations in or near a highly desirable location, close to public transportation, nearby attractions, or where guests will want to visit (plus onsite or nearby parking is available.)

▶ Extra amenities, beyond clean sheets and towels, are provided by the host to help set the accommodations apart from the competition. How to choose the best selection of amenities to offer is also covered within Chapter 4.

▶ A truly unique or unusual accommodation experience that guests are willing to pay a premium for.

warning ⚠

If you opt to charge an extra cleaning fee, which is your prerogative as a host with Airbnb, your guests will expect professionally cleaned accommodations.

For each guest that you host, their experience will include a series of phases that begin once someone finds your listing on the Airbnb website or mobile app. When your listing catches someone's attention, the potential guest will make contact with you via the website or app. It's important that you, as the host, respond promptly and accurately to inquiries, always maintaining a friendly and professional attitude.

Once the reservation is made, as the host, it's your responsibility to clean and prepare the accommodations for each guest's arrival. Everything should be set up and waiting for them before they arrive. It's essential that the description of the property that you provided on the Airbnb service, and the amenities you said were included, are all accurate and ready for your guests upon their arrival.

After you've agreed to an arrival time with your guest, you, or an approved representative, will typically need to be on-hand to welcome the guest, present them with the keys, review the house rules, provide a tour, and get them settled in.

► As a Host, Stay in Touch with Your Guests

As the host, it's your responsibility to check in with your guests periodically during their stay and make sure they have everything they need. Also, be sure you're available to answer their questions, address their concerns, and ensure their overall experience is as positive as possible.

Keep in mind that when it comes to writing reviews and ratings, guests who have something bad to say are more apt to post a review and rating than someone who has something positive to stay based on their overall good experience staying with you. The ratings and reviews you receive as a host are very important, so it's essential you take steps to ensure the best possible reactions from your guests.

During your guest's stay, it's up to you and them in terms of how much interaction you actually have. As you'll learn, some hosts opt to socialize with their guests, share meals, take on the role of tour guide, and have a lot of day-to-day interaction with their guests. Others remain available in-person, by phone, email, or text message, but give their guests more freedom and autonomy. Your involvement and level of interaction with your guests will be based on your own personal preference, as well as the wants and needs of your guests.

Depending on the type of accommodations you're offering, your geographic location, competition, demand, and seasonal trends, for example, you may find that you're able to keep your accommodations booked night after night, with short-term, mid-term, or even long-term guests. This means that for every night one or more people are staying at your property, you'll be earning money.

More realistically, especially for new Airbnb hosts in geographic areas that are not popular tourist destinations, you can expect guests to book your accommodations less often. This might mean you'll have guests sporadically throughout each month.

Based on your goals, this book will demonstrate many proven strategies for attracting the attention of guests using the Airbnb service (as well as similar services). However, if you're offering accommodations in an undesirable geographic location, or what you're offering does not meet the needs of most Airbnb travelers, don't expect to receive consistent bookings, even if you have top-notch reviews and ratings.

One thing you can be sure about, however, is that if you start receiving negative feedback and ratings from your guests, it will become harder and harder for you as a host to generate bookings, as guests who are savvy using the Airbnb service will know to seek out accommodations that have received better reviews and ratings from past guests.

► As a Host, You Need to Meet or Exceed the Expectations of Your Guests

Throughout this book, and within the interviews of successful travel hosts, the concept of offering a clean, comfortable, and safe place to stay is emphasized heavily and repeatedly. As a prospective Airbnb host, if you're unwilling or unable to offer this, don't bother to become a host. It's that simple. Offering dirty, uncomfortable, or otherwise uninhabitable accommodations will lead to bad reviews and ratings, which will deter future guests from booking with you.

As you create your profile and listing on Airbnb, or whatever service you opt to use, you want to be positive, but also honest, and back up the description of your property with clear, detailed, and professional-looking photographs. It's important that you set realistic expectations for your guests, based on what you're offering and how much you're charging. Total accuracy within your online profile and property listing is absolutely essential.

First and foremost, guests want a clean place to stay! This means that the bedrooms and bathroom(s) should be spotless, fully functional, and comfortable, and the bedding (sheets, blankets, pillows, etc.), as well as the towels that you provide, should be all clean, odor free, freshly laundered, and stain free.

Depending on how much you're charging, and the expectations you create within your Airbnb profile and listing, guests will typically expect their accommodations to be cleaned and prepared prior to their arrival. For example, if they're being offered access to a kitchen, for example, the dishes, countertops, and appliances should be clean and ready to use. The beds should be made (with clean bedding), and the bathroom should have clean towels, toilet paper, and other necessities (soap and perhaps shampoo) available and ready to use.

Most guests will understand that they're saving money by staying in a private residence, as opposed to a hotel with professional and on-call housekeepers and front desk personnel, for example. However, these same guests will also have basic expectations that it becomes your obligation as a host to meet or exceed. This relates to the actual accommodations you're providing, as well as your attitude, friendliness, and helpfulness that you offer as a host before and during each guest's stay with you.

So, lesson one for being a successful Airbnb host is to set realistic expectations for your guests, set a fair nightly price based on what you're offering, and then do whatever is in your power as the host to meet or exceed the expectations you've set via your online profile and listing.

Some Airbnb hosts generate enough money to cover some or all of their mortgage payment or monthly rent, as well as extras like utility bills and real estate taxes. There are also some people who have been able to earn enough money to support themselves exclusively as an Airbnb host.

But realistically, becoming an Airbnb host is *not* a continuous and reliable revenue stream that you should count on, at least initially, until based on what you're offering, your personal experience as an Airbnb host proves otherwise. For the majority of Airbnb hosts, having guests stay at their property offers a secondary and sporadic revenue stream that gives them extra money to help cover their bills or improve their lifestyle.

Don't Be Impulsive!

When you visit the website for Airbnb or any similar service, you're encouraged to immediately start setting up your profile so you can become a host. Before taking this step, however, finish reading this book, learn more about what you're getting involved in, and, most importantly, make sure you're legally allowed to serve as a host based on where you live.

A growing number of cities around the world no longer allow private home, apartment, or condo owners to participate on these services or allow paid guests to stay within their homes. Thus, it's illegal to have paying guests for fewer than 30 days, unless the property is locally licensed as a hotel or bed-and-breakfast, for example.

Some cities that allow home, apartment, or condo owners to utilize their property for short-term rentals, or accommodate paying nightly guests, require hosts acquire a special permit or business license. Failure to comply with local laws could result in hefty fines.

Meanwhile, if you're not hindered by local laws or regulations, you may discover that your homeowner's association, coop board, or landlord forbids participation in this type of service as a host. Many apartment leases, for example, do not permit short-term rentals or sublets of any kind, and a violation of the lease could lead to eviction by the landlord. Check with your landlord, homeowner's association, or coop board before you register and start offering your apartment, home, or condo as a short-term rental or allow paying guests to stay in your home.

If you live in rent-controlled or subsidized housing, there will likely be limitations on what you're allowed to do in terms of participation as a host on services like Airbnb. Check with your property manager, and carefully review your lease or rental agreement.

The Airbnb website offers a section that covers legal requirements and restrictions in about 50 U.S. cities (see www.airbnb.com/help/article/1376/responsible-hosting-in-the-united-states). However, it's ultimately your responsibility to determine what's legal and permissible in your local city or community. One way to do this is to check with the state or local government. For example, check with your city town hall, the city's zoning board, and/or the local housing authority.

If from a legal standpoint you're freely able to become a host with Airbnb or a similar service, because you are earning money from this activity, you're expected to pay federal and state income taxes on this revenue. In some cases you may also be required to pay an ongoing hotel/transient occupancy tax or sales tax, for example. It's a good idea to have a conversation with your accountant to determine what tax implications becoming a host will have for you personally and how this additional income could impact your tax-filing procedures.

Once you determine that being an Airbnb host (or a host with a similar service) is permissible, also have a discussion with your insurance provider. Make sure that you have the necessary insurance coverage related to liability and property protection. Do not rely on promises made by any service that states that its hosts, the host's family members, their pets, as well as their property and belongings, are fully covered and insured. In many situations, this is not the case, despite what hosts are led to believe.

► Use Common Sense to Avoid Potential Problems

Every business opportunity attracts its share of scam artists and criminals. Overall, Airbnb (and similar services) offers a credible and viable way for hosts to earn money by inviting guests to stay on their property for a nightly fee. Out of the millions of transactions between hosts and guests that take place around the world on a daily basis, a small percentage involves guests (or in some cases, hosts) perpetuating some type of scam or illegal activity.

Throughout this book, you'll discover tips and strategies for identifying and avoiding potentially problematic guests. However, as a host, it's a good idea to stay informed about the types of scams being perpetrated. This is not something that Airbnb (or any other service) will necessarily advise you of or protect you against.

One way to find out about these scams, and how they're evolving over time, is simply to access any internet search engine, and within the search field, type "Airbnb scams." Then, click on the search results from credible sources, such as news agencies you know.

As you'll discover, simply by using common sense and taking a few basic steps to protect yourself, your belongings, and your property, chances are you'll be able to avoid problems as a host.

Hosting Options Beyond Airbnb

It's important to understand that as a potential host, you have options beyond working exclusively with Airbnb. In some cases, you may find it advantageous to work with multiple services and promote your property on two or more services simultaneously in order to reach the broadest possible audience.

You may discover, however, that based on what you're offering, one or more of these other services better cater to your needs or the types of travelers you want to attract as guests. To help you quickly get started with your research, listed here alphabetically are ten other services you'll see referred to throughout this book:

1. *FlipKey (www.flipkey.com).* Operated by TripAdvisor (www.tripadvisor.com), this service features more than 3,000 vacation homes and rooms located throughout the world. Every host/property owner is verified by the service, which also relies heavily on reviews and ratings to help travelers choose the perfect and most affordable accommodations based on their needs.

2. *HomeAway (www.homeaway.com).* Owned and operated by the popular Expedia (www.expedia.com) travel service, HomeAway features more than 1.2 million vacation home rental listings, located in more than 190 countries. This service helps property owners/landlords find short-term paying guests to stay at their second home/vacation property and handles all online bookings. The goal of this service is to help travelers find spacious and private accommodations, for less money than a traditional hotel.

3. *HomeSuite (www.yourhomesuite.com).* As you'll learn from the company's CEO David Adams later in this book, this service matches up tens of thousands of home and apartment owners/landlords with guests looking for accommodations for between 30 days and up to one year. (This service does not handle short-term rentals.) Each property is vetted by HomeSuite prior to being listed on the service. The company currently operates in San Francisco, Los Angeles, New York City, Washington, DC, Chicago, Seattle, Boston, San Diego, Houston, and Dallas, and is continuously expanding into other major U.S. cities.

4. *Kid & Coe (www.kidandcoe.com).* This service works exclusively with a selection of more than 850 curated and verified hosts around the world that offer stand-alone, family-friendly homes as short-term rental properties.

5. *Onefinestay (www.onefinestay.com).* Offering high-end rental homes in London, Los Angeles, New York City, Paris, Rome, and a few other cities around the world, onefinestay works with a select group of property owners/landlords to offer travelers accommodations in homes that offer a consistent set of amenities. According

to the service, for a home to be considered for inclusion on the service, it must offer "space, character, and comfort." Unlike similar services, onefinestay creates the listing and takes the photographs related to each featured home, handles all reservations, and offers each guest an in-person welcome.

6. *Roomorama (www.roomorama.com).* This online service allows travelers to book short-term vacation rentals and accommodations around the world from a pool of verified hosts. The service currently works with more than 80,000 owner-managed and professionally managed properties worldwide.

7. *Travelmob (www.travelmob.com).* This service operates much like Airbnb, but is based in Singapore, and works with hosts offering single rooms or complete apartments or homes throughout the Asia/Pacific region. Targeted to tourists, Travelmob allows guests to immerse themselves in the local culture of their destination and have an authentic travel experience that they would not otherwise get staying at a typical hotel. Travelmob was acquired by HomeAway, Inc. in 2013, but operates as a separate service.

8. *Tripping (www.tripping.com).* This service boasts that it offers the world's largest search engine for short-term rentals and vacation homes, because it allows travelers to compare accommodations available across some of the world's top rental sites, such as HomeAway, VRBO, TripAdvisor, HouseTrip, Interhome, Roomorama, and Booking. As a result, travelers can quickly browse through more than eight million private accommodation options around the world, with prices ranging from $10.00 to $10,000 per night. Property offerings include furnished homes, beach houses, ski cabins, oceanfront mansions, and modern apartments located in the heart of the world's most popular cities. This service offers only opportunities where travelers can reserve the entire apartment, condo, or home, as opposed to having the host living on-site, or guests having to share the space with other guests.

9. *VacationRentals (www.vacationrentals.com).* As part of the "HomeAway family," this service helps property owners and managers list and promote their properties and handles all reservations and payments via its website and mobile app. The biggest reason why property owners utilize this service is to help them cover the cost of ownership by renting to travelers.

10. *VRBO (Vacation Rentals by Owner, www.vrbo.com).* Also part of the HomeAway family of services, VRBO allows property owners/landlords to list their entire home, condo, villa, cabin, castle, chalet, cottage, or mansion on the service as a short-term rental opportunity. The website is visited by more than 44 million travelers every month. Individual guestroom or shared home/apartment listings,

or listings where the hosts lives on-site within the property are not accepted. The typical person using this site will be traveling with friends or family members and requires multiple bedrooms and bathrooms. According to VRBO, the top 5 percent of its hosts/property owners wind up earning up to $88,000 per year.

In addition to the many services that allow hosts to charge guests a nightly fee for accommodations, there's also Couchsurfing (www.couchsurfing.com), which is a free service for hosts and travelers. Instead of offering guests an entire room, however, hosts are only required to offer guests a couch or air mattress to sleep on. This is more of a social experience that allows hosts to meet new people and potentially make friends, because there is no income-earning potential.

Airbnb Is Evolving as a Travel Service

Originally, the Airbnb.com online service and mobile apps were simply used to help travelers find and book interesting places to stay. In November 2016, however, Airbnb started to evolve into a full-service travel site that focuses on allowing travelers to learn about and book travel experiences—not just accommodations. Airbnb users can now choose a travel destination, find accommodations, and, at the same time, learn about (and make reservations for) unique experiences.

This new functionality is referred to as Airbnb Trips. According to a press release issued by Airbnb (https://press.atairbnb.com/airbnb-expands-beyond-the-home-with-the-launch-of-trips), this new service, "Brings together where you stay, what you do, and the people you meet, all in one place. Trips is a people-platform designed to make travel both easy and magical."

As of early 2017, Airbnb's focus is on experiences, places, and homes. Soon, travelers will also be able to book flights and travel-related services, which will ultimately transform Airbnb.com into a full-service travel website, like Travelocity.com, Priceline.com, Orbitz. com, or Expedia.com, for example.

As an Airbnb host, additional opportunities are (or will soon be) available that allow you to share your expertise or passions, to provide unique experiences to travelers, in addition to accommodations. At launch, Airbnb Trips was offered in 12 cities around the world, with rapid expansion planned in 2017 and beyond.

Now that you have a basic understanding of what's involved in becoming a travel host, let's take a closer look at how to get started as a host with Airbnb. This is the focus of Chapter 2, "Get Started as an Airbnb Host."

Get Started as an Airbnb Host

One of the first steps required when joining Airbnb or a similar service is to create a personal profile and a listing for your property on the website.

Before you can effectively promote your service, it's important to do an honest self-assessment and a thorough analysis of your property. This is an opportunity to promote what you have to offer and why potential guests should stay with you.

Determine Exactly What You Have to Offer to Your Future Guests

It's important to establish what you're willing to offer related to your property. Your options may include:

▶ A single private room within your home

▶ A shared room within your home

▶ Your entire home or apartment

▶ A special type of property, such as a guesthouse, cabin, ski chalet, treehouse, castle, studio apartment, multifloor apartment, finished basement, private island, oceanfront villa, loft, townhouse, boat/yacht, or bungalow

Next, determine why people will want to stay with you and what you can promote within your property listing in order to get their attention. In addition to promoting that you offer a clean, safe, and comfortable living space (which is typically the bare minimum of what potential guests look for), figure out what exactly you're able to offer that will make your property extra appealing.

tip

Look at other property listings (and photos) on Airbnb to determine what aspect of each listing catches your attention and why. What is it about each listing that would make you want to stay there? If something turns you off about a listing, determine what that is, and don't make the same mistake when creating your own listing.

▶ Do Your Research and Determine Why Superhosts Have Become Successful

Before you start creating your own personal profile and property listing on Airbnb, investigate your competition on Airbnb, and carefully read the profiles and property listings created by already successful Airbnb hosts and Superhosts in your geographic area and elsewhere. You can easily find the successful hosts by looking at the number of positive ratings they've received and by looking for the Superhost badge that accompanies their profile and property listing.

A Superhost is an experienced Airbnb host who has hosted at least ten separate guests within the past year; at least 80 percent of their reviews are five stars; their response rate when it comes to communicating with potential guests is 90 percent or higher; and as a host, they honor their confirmed reservations (with very few or zero cancelations).

Some of the key things potential guests might look for include:

▶ *Your geographic location.* How close is your property to popular tourist attractions, landmarks, special events happening in your area, and/or public transportation? What's desirable about the location?

▶ *Available value-added services.* Things like on-site or nearby parking, laundry facilities, or being walking distance to local shopping or restaurants are always a plus.

▶ *Amenities you offer.* Being able to offer your guests a private, clean, and fully functional bathroom (as opposed to a shared bathroom) is often appreciated by potential guests. There are countless other amenities you definitely should offer, as well as additional and optional amenities that your guests will likely appreciate. Choosing the best selection of amenities is covered a bit later. For now, understand that your offerings are among the factors that will attract potential guests to select your property when they're choosing a place to stay.

▶ *Your commitment as a host.* Are you willing to prepare meals for or dine with your guests, act as a tour guide, or socialize with your guests? Beyond the bare minimums of what's expected from a host, what else will you offer?

In short, ask yourself, what makes your property so special or unique? Why will people want to stay with you? These are two of the most important questions you'll need to address, promote, and showcase within your Airbnb heading, property listing, photos, and personal profile.

Your Airbnb Personal Profile and Property Listing Should Reveal a Lot About You

One of the key reasons why Airbnb works as an online community is because hosts and guests alike are asked to create their own personal profile, which is publically displayed on the service. Potential guests can look at a host's profile, in addition to their property listing(s), to help make a more educated decision about where to stay. Meanwhile, hosts can review the profile of each prospective guest before making a decision about whether or not to accept a requested reservation.

Your online presence with Airbnb has the following important components:

▶ Your personal profile
▶ One or more photographs of you
▶ Your property listing

- ▶ Photographs that showcase your property
- ▶ Your personal ratings/reviews
- ▶ Your property's ratings/reviews

Your personal profile introduces you as a person to potential guests and includes a list of identification/contact-related details that have been verified by Airbnb. After Airbnb identifies your identity, your profile will automatically receive and display a "Verified" badge, which helps to enhance your credibility on the service.

As a host, the contact information you provide (such as your phone number, email address, and Facebook page URL) is not revealed to potential guests until after they've booked and paid for a reservation to stay with you. The driver's license information you provide to Airbnb when creating your profile is never revealed to others but is listed as a form of "verified ID" that Airbnb has received.

Your profile page also includes photos of you, details about where you're from, how long you've been a member of Airbnb, and a summary of your reviews. Guests often build up a collection of personal reviews that will also be displayed as part of your profile.

The About Me section of your profile can include additional at-a-glance information about you, such as where you went to school, what you do for work, what languages you speak, as well as information about your interests and hobbies. Ideally, the information you provide can make you come across as more appealing to potential guests who share things in common with you.

As a host based in the United States, if you're fluent in French, for example, and you promote this within your profile, travelers visiting the United States from France may be more inclined to stay with you because you speak their language.

Keep in mind that every piece of information that's requested by Airbnb to include in your personal profile or property listing can help you showcase yourself and your property in a positive way, based on the information you choose to provide. While you always have the option to refrain from sharing certain pieces of requested information, the more forthcoming you are, the easier it will be for potential guests to virtually get to know you, so you can begin building credibility and trust before you begin communicating with or actually meet potential guests.

warning

Your profile page includes a summary of both the reviews you have received as a host, as well as those you have received as a guest during your own travels. Someone can use information offered by both sets of reviews to draw conclusions about you. If you're rude, messy, and unreliable as a guest, once you become a host, these reviews will be viewable by your potential guests.

Create Your Airbnb Account

There are three main tasks involved in establishing an Airbnb host account:

1. Sign up for the service
2. Create a profile
3. Create a listing

These are discussed in the following sections. Once you complete the steps, you can expand your profile to include additional information, plus create a detailed property listing.

The remainder of the chapter will walk you through the process of creating a personal profile and then a property listing on Airbnb. However, keep in mind that the Airbnb website and mobile app are constantly evolving, so the order in which information is requested, and the steps involved in actually creating the profile and listing, will vary slightly when you do this. As you go through this process, be sure to provide the information that's requested in a succinct and accurate way.

Sign Up for the Service

Signing up needs to be done only once and takes just a few minutes to complete, but plan on spending much more time when creating and fine-tuning your profile and property listing.

1. Go to www.airbnb.com and click the Sign Up button that's displayed near the top-right corner of the homepage. If you're using an iPhone or iPad (or an Android-based smartphone or tablet), download the app to your device, launch the app, and from the opening screen, tap on the Create Account button in order to begin creating your personal profile. The free Airbnb app is available from the App Store (iPhone/iPad) or Google Play App Store (Android).

2. Select one of the following three options:
   ▶ Continue with Facebook
   ▶ Continue with Google
   ▶ Sign up with Email

3. If you choose Facebook or Google, you'll need to grant permission to Airbnb so it can access the appropriate account information.

4. If you choose the Sign up with Email option, you'll be prompted to fill the First Name, Last Name, Email Address, and Date of Birth fields and then create a password for your account.

5. After filling in the fields, click the Sign Up button to establish the free account. You'll be asked to accept Airbnb's commitment to respect and include everyone in the Airbnb community. You will then see the "Welcome to Airbnb" message.

6. Click on the Get Started button to continue. You can now create a profile.

Create Your Airbnb Personal Profile

In the future, you simply need to log in to the website (or mobile app) using your email address and password that you just used to set up the account. Otherwise, you'll use your Facebook or Google account details to log in.

Add Photos

Click the Get Started button and you'll be prompted to add a profile photo to your account. At this point, upload a digital photo you have of yourself that's stored on your computer or that you've previously published on Facebook. Select the Upload Photo or Use Facebook Photo option, and then follow the on-screen prompts to add your personal photo to the account.

Add and Confirm Your Phone Number

After uploading a photo, you'll be prompted to enter and confirm your phone number. Type your mobile phone number, and then click on the Confirm Phone Number button. Keep in mind that this is the phone number that will ultimately be provided to the hosts you opt to stay with as a guest, as well as to your guests with a paid reservation once you become a host. The phone number is not publically displayed as part of your profile. When Airbnb needs to send you text messages, this will be the number that's used (unless you change it later by updating your profile).

Within a few seconds after submitting your mobile phone number, you will receive a text message from Airbnb with a four-digital security code. Enter this code into the appropriate field within the Airbnb website when prompted.

Confirm Your Email Address

Click the Confirm Email button that's embedded in the email you receive. If you linked your Facebook page or Google account with your Airbnb account, Airbnb will access your email address from your account details. At this point you can explore the Airbnb service

tip

Select personal photos for your profile where you are smiling and look friendly. After all, the photo(s) people see in your profile will be their first impression of you. It's important to select and use photos in your personal profile that clearly show your face.

as a guest or click the Become a Host button to begin the process of becoming an Airbnb host. Regardless of which option to choose, spend a few additional minutes to add more information to your personal profile before moving on.

Add Additional Profile Information

To add more information to your personal profile, click your username/photo, which is now displayed near the top-right corner of the Airbnb.com website's main page and follow these steps:

1. Click the Edit Profile option. From the Edit Profile screen, fill in the additional fields that allow you to share additional information about yourself. For example, click on the Gender field, and select Male or Female.

2. If you wish to add an additional phone number to your account, click the +Add a Phone Number option that's displayed below the Phone Number field. The original phone number you provided should now have a Confirmed message associated with it.

3. Click on the Preferred Language field to select your native language, and then click on the Preferred Currency pull-down menu to select USD (United States Dollars) if you're based in the United States.

4. Within the Where You Live field, include your city, state, and country, such as "Los Angeles, California, USA." Do not include your street address at this time.

5. Click on the field associated with the Describe Yourself option, and use this space to provide information that will help people get to know you. For example, explain what it's like (or will be like) to have you as a host, what activities you enjoy, and provide any additional information about your lifestyle, personality, education, hobbies, personal philosophies, and/or travel experiences that people might find interesting about you. If you're at a loss for what to say, take a few minutes to review the profiles of other Airbnb hosts. Also, ask a few of your best friends what qualities they most like about you, and then consider sharing that information as well.

6. Under the Optional heading, fill in the School field with information about your education. This is optional information, but sharing additional information about yourself will help people get to know you and feel more comfortable with you as a host. Include details about where and when you went to high school and/or college and what degree(s) you've earned, for example.

7. In the Work field, include information about the type of work you do as your primary job. Here, you can be as broad or specific as you desire.

8. Next, click on the Time Zone field, and select the time zone where you live (and where your property is located).

9. Click on the Languages option if you fluently speak additional languages, and list them one at a time. The more languages you're able to add, the more desirable you'll be as a host among international travelers.

10. Use the Emergency Contact field to provide details about someone whom Airbnb can contact in case of an emergency related to you or your property, for example. This is information that only Airbnb has access to; it's not actually displayed within your profile.

11. Click on the Shipping Address field to include your detailed mailing address. This information is used if Airbnb needs to mail you something. It can be different from your property address, or a P.O. box, for example.

12. If you travel for business (work-related purposes) and might want to stay at Airbnb properties as part of your business trips instead of utilizing traditional hotels, fill in your work email address in the field provided below the Business Travel heading.

Once you've filled in all of the required fields and any optional ones, click the Save button to save your changes and update your profile. Confirm your password when prompted. At this point, you can also add photos and videos and start the Verification ID process via the menu to left of the Edit Profile information.

Photos, Videos, and the Verification ID

Click on the Photos, Symbol, and Video option to add additional personal profile photos to your account, associate a symbol or logo with your profile, and to upload an optional personal video that introduces yourself.

Click on the Trust and Verification option to participate in Airbnb's Verified ID process. This requires you to share a copy of your government-issued ID (such as a driver's license) with Airbnb, plus link your personal social media accounts (such as your Facebook, Google, and/or LinkedIn accounts) with your Airbnb profile in a way that allows Airbnb to verify this information. You're also able to link your American Express credit card with your account as part of the verification process.

warning

Honesty is important. If you're caught falsifying information within your profile, people who write reviews about you in the future will definitely point this out, and your credibility will be tarnished.

Verifying your ID needs to be done only once and a Verified ID badge will be displayed as part of your personal profile when you complete the process. The more verifications you have listed on your profile, the more credible you appear.

Many hosts require their guests to have a Verified ID with Airbnb prior to accepting a reservation. As a host, however, having a Verified ID is ultimately a requirement. Again, the more pieces of information that Airbnb is able to verify, the better this will look when someone views your profile. While the verified information itself is not shared, your profile will say that your driver's license, phone number, email address, Facebook page, and your LinkedIn account, for example, have been verified.

Once you begin using Airbnb as a traveler or host, the ratings and reviews you receive will automatically be added to your profile. Note that potential guests will appreciate one additional piece of information in your personal profile: optional references.

Optional References

Click on the References option, and then follow the screen prompts in order to request references from your personal friends or business associates. References should be written by people who know you well, such as personal friends or people you work with. Your parents, spouse, kids, or other relatives are not the best references to use in this situation.

To have the Airbnb service request references from people you know on your behalf, from below the Email Your Friends heading, enter the email addresses, one at a time, for the people Airbnb should contact. Those people will receive an email from Airbnb asking them to provide a text-based reference on your behalf. This information, once it's received by Airbnb, will automatically become part of your personal profile and viewable by anyone who reads your profile.

Again, the more information you share within your profile, the easier it will be for your potential guest to get to know you and quickly feel comfortable with the idea of potentially staying at your property.

Create Your Airbnb Property Listing

After you've created your Airbnb personal profile, the next step is to create a listing for your property. To do this, return to the Airbnb website, sign into your account, and click on the Become a Host button.

Then you'll need to provide the following information to complete your property listing:

tip

You may ultimately need to create and manage multiple property listings on Airbnb if you'll be renting out more than one separate bedroom within your property (potentially to different guests) or if you have multiple properties to promote.

1. Basic information about the property, including details about the number of bedrooms, bathrooms, beds, and amenities you're offering.

2. Photos of the property, and add a title and text-based description of your property. The title is one of the first things potential guests will see, so it's important that your title be descriptive, concise, attention-grabbing, and accurate and that it sets your property apart from other Airbnb listings. Give the wording of your title some extra thought, and be creative.

3. Set a nightly price, list the dates when your property is available, and customize a handful of booking-related settings.

4. Add optional items, including a Host Guidebook, which explains some of the points of interest, restaurants, and activities that are close to your property that potential guests might be interested in.

Step 1: Provide Your Basic Information

Click on the Become a Host option. Under the Step 1 heading, click on the Continue button to proceed. Then select the type of property you're listing. Your options include: Entire Place, Private Room, or Shared Room. Choose the option that best describes what you'll be offering as a host. Click on the Next button to proceed.

Following are some of the additional questions you'll be asked about your property:

▶ *How many guests can your place accommodate?* Enter how many beds you have to offer, the types of beds they are, and the total number of guests that can stay at once.

▶ *How many bathrooms?* Enter the number of bathrooms your property contains and whether the bathrooms are private or shared.

▶ Keep Your Profile and Property Listing Up to Date

Once you create and publish your property listing, you can always go back onto the Airbnb website to tweak or fine-tune the listing, based on feedback you receive from guests or improvements you've made to the property, for example. If you've purchased a new mattress or brand-new bedding or have begun offering additional amenities, these are definite reasons to update your property listing.

It's a good strategy to get into the habit of updating your property listing at least once every month or two, to ensure it's up to date and describes the most compelling reasons why potential guests should stay with you.

▶ *Where's your place located?* Provide your complete address, including the house and/or apartment number, as appropriate. Only confirmed guests, with a pre-paid reservation, will receive your exact address. This information is not displayed as part of your public profile or listing. On the map that's displayed, if necessary, drag the virtual pushpin to the exact location of your property. Based on the address you entered, the Google Map that's displayed should be able to pinpoint your address rather accurately, however.

▶ *What amenities do you offer?* From the list that's provided, check the box for each amenity listing that applies. You'll have the opportunity to describe other amenities later.

▶ *What spaces can guests use?* Based on all of the rooms/areas included within your property, check the boxes associated with which area(s) your guests will be able to freely utilize. Your options include: Kitchen, Laundry (washer/dryer), Parking, Elevator, Pool, Hot Tub, and Gym. You'll be able to describe other areas within your property that guests will have access to later, if applicable.

aha!

Taking proper photos is a time-consuming and detail-oriented task. Be sure to clean and prepare your property before photographing it. Remember, you can always click on the Remind Me Later option, finish composing your listing, and then go back and spend the time needed to take and edit your photos before actually publishing your listing online.

While you can use the camera that's built into your smartphone or tablet to snap some photos, you will likely achieve more professional-quality results if you use a higher-end, high-resolution digital camera.

Step 2: Share Photos and Add a Titled Description

Take photos of your property and the room(s) where your guests will be staying. Show as much detail as possible, and try to make your photos as professional looking as possible. Thus, proper lighting is important. See the section, "Strategies for Adding Attention-Grabbing Photos to Your Listing," for more information about taking and editing digital photos that properly showcase your property.

Now, create your property description. When prompted, fill in the following fields:

▶ *My place is close to.* Enter any points of interest, tourist attractions, or other geographic locations that your potential guests may find appealing. For example, if you're walking distance to public transportation, list this. Some options you can

▶ Strategies for Adding Attention-Grabbing Photos to Your Listing

What you say within your listing is important; however, the visual images of your property (the photos) that you showcase will ultimately play a huge role in the decision-making process for your prospective guests. Thus, it's essential that your photos truly showcase your property in the best possible way. This applies to Airbnb hosts, as well as anyone offering their property through any short-term rental service. Whichever service you opt to use as a host, your property photos are extremely important.

While your prospective guests might spend a few minutes reading your personal profile and property listing, it'll be the photos of your property (and your personal profile photos) that play a major role in someone's decision to book a reservation to stay at your property.

You've probably heard the saying that a picture is worth a thousand words. When it comes to photos within your Airbnb property listing, this is a very true statement. Offer prospective guests a collection of photos that truly showcases your property. Show them the outside as well as specific areas within the property they'll be utilizing, such as the bedroom(s), bathroom(s), kitchen, patio, and/or living room area.

Remember, you want to communicate visually that your property is clean and comfortable, so stage and capture your property in a way that showcases this in the best possible way. The following are a few tips for taking the best possible photos:

▶ *Use the highest-resolution camera you can.* If you're using a smartphone or tablet's built-in camera, use the rear-facing camera, which allows you to take higher-resolution photos.

▶ *Use natural lighting.* Shine as much natural light into each room as possible, and try to avoid using the camera's flash. Capturing natural, ambient light will make the property look more appealing.

▶ *Clean up before taking your photos.* Showcase photos that present your property exactly how guests will discover it when they arrive. Remove personal items or clutter from each room before taking your pictures.

▶ *Showcase what's unique or special about your property.* Be sure to highlight any special or appealing amenities, such as a big-screen TV, hot tub, kitchen, or patio that your guests will enjoy using.

► **Strategies,** continued

    ► *Include a selection of both interior and exterior shots.* If you live in an area that experiences distinct seasons, update your photos in the future to showcase the current season.

    ► *Study what others have done.* In addition to reviewing photos presented in other Airbnb property listings, take a look at photos of homes/apartments being sold. Notice how each room is "staged" to look clean, uncluttered, and homelike. Try to replicate this approach to visually convey as much information about your property as possible within your photos.

    ► *Determine the best order in which your photos get displayed on the Airbnb website and mobile app.* Showcase the most appealing aspects of your property first, keeping in mind that guests want to see where they'll be sleeping and spending most of their time while staying with you.

    ► *Showcase the bedrooms.* Make the beds, and highlight the clean pillows, sheets, and blankets you offer. Also be sure that other furniture in the room is presented nicely, including nightstands, dressers, etc.

    ► *Showcase the bathroom.* Make sure the shower/bathtub, toilet, and sink areas are all visible and appear very clean. Towels should be folded and presented neatly on a shelf or towel rack within the photo(s). No mold, mildew, soap scum, or dirty laundry should appear in these photos. Your potential guests will want to see a clean and sanitary bathroom that will provide them with privacy when it's in use.

Consider hiring a professional photographer to photograph your home. Yes, you may need to pay for photography services upfront, but the results will be worth it and will help your property listing positively stand out on Airbnb. The Airbnb service can help you find a professional photographer in your area to work with for free (visit www.airbnb.com/info/photography), or you can easily find a talented photographer on your own and then pay for their services.

choose from include: Art and Culture, Great Views, Restaurants and Dining, the Beach, and/or Family-Friendly Activities. Click on any of these options, or type whatever is appropriate.

► *You'll love my place because of.* Type the most prevalent reasons why someone will want to stay at your property. This might include a brief description of the ambiance or something special that your property offers that hasn't been listed elsewhere. In addition to typing text into the provided field, you can choose from these options: the Views, the Location, the People, the Ambiance, or the Outdoor Space.

▶ *My place is good for.* Check each box that applies to the type of traveler who will enjoy and be comfortable staying at your property. Your options include: Couples, Solo Adventurers, Business Travelers, Families (with Kids), Big Groups, and Furry Friends (Pets).

Based on your responses to these, the Airbnb website will draft a text-based, paragraph-long description of your property. You can leave this description as is, but to get the most attention from potential guests, take a few minutes to edit the text to be more customized to what specifically you're offering and who you're offering it to. You can utilize up to 500 characters in the Edit Your Description field.

tip

The Edit Your Description field is a great place to promote what's truly special or unique about your property and to emphasize that you're offering a clean, comfortable, and safe place to stay. If you're targeting solo travelers, couples, business travelers, or families, for example, explain exactly why your property will instantly appeal to a specific type of traveler.

The Name Your Place field is where you'll compose your listing's title. It can be up to 50 characters long. Write something that is descriptive and attention-getting and that will appeal to your target guest.

At this point, you can preview your listing and see exactly how it will appear on the Airbnb website and within the mobile app. Click OK and then Continue. If you haven't already done so, go back and upload your property photos. Do not actually publish your Airbnb property listing without adding photos.

Step 3: Set Your Rate and Availability Dates

Before you set your rate and available dates there are few preliminary items to tend to. First, you'll be prompted to answer the following questions:

▶ *Have you rented out your place before?* Your options include: I Have or I'm New to This.

▶ *How often do you want to have guests?* Your options include: As Often as Possible, Part-time, or Not Sure Yet.

The Settings screen lists three separate options: Calendar, Trip Length, and Availability.

▶ Calendar provides month-to-month calendars and the option to manually block out specific dates that your property will *not* be available to guests.

▶ The Trip Length option sets the minimum and maximum number of consecutive nights a guest can book your property for. Some hosts set a two-night minimum, for example, while others allow guests to book for as little as one night. For the maximum nights, you can set this to any number that's higher than your minimum night stay. As a new host, you might want to keep the maximum stay short (a week or less), so you don't wind up with someone staying at your property for a long period, if you happen to decide against remaining a host.

▶ The Availability screen offers three options you can customize, including: Advance Notice, Preparation Time, and Booking Window. These options allow you to fine-tine when your property will be available for bookings, based on a series of personal preferences and the time needed for cleaning, for example.

• Use Advance Notice to set the number of days in advance guests must book and pre-pay for their reservation prior to their arrival. The default option is Same Day, meaning that they can book a reservation and begin staying with you that same day. As a new host, you might require one day advance notice to give you ample time to prepare your property and communicate with the potential guests.

• Use Preparation Time to choose how much time in between reservations you need to clean your property and prepare it for the next guest. Your options include: No Prep Time, One Day, or Two Days. Airbnb will automatically adjust your property's availability based on booked reservations and the time you say is needed between them.

• Use Booking to determine how far in advance someone can book a reservation. Your options include: Any Time, Three Months, Six Months, or One Year.

warning

Remember, once you accept a booking/ reservation as a host, you are penalized and will receive negative ratings/ reviews if you later cancel on a guest. Don't accept any reservation that you don't plan to honor.

Now you can actually set a nightly price, but be sure to do some research. First, explore the Airbnb website (or mobile app), and figure out what other hosts with comparable properties in your area are charging. Next, go online or call nearby hotels, motels, B&Bs, and/or resorts, and determine what their nightly pricing is.

When setting your own nightly rate, you have two options. You can choose the Price Adapts to Demand

tip

As a new host, you'll likely wind up wanting or needing to tweak your nightly pricing as you receive feedback from your initial guests and read their reviews related to the value of what you're offering. Likewise, if you improve your property or add new amenities, you'll probably want to update your pricing to reflect this.

option or the Price Is Fixed option. If you select the first, adaptive option, you will be asked to set a fixed price and a price range. Then, the Airbnb service will automatically adjust your price. When local demand is high, your nighty rate will automatically be promoted as being higher.

If you select the Price Is Fixed option, this means that you set a nightly rate, and that rate will always be in effect, unless you manually change it. Regardless of which option you choose, the Airbnb service will offer tips to help you choose the best nightly fixed price or price range, based on what you're offering, your geographic location, and seasonal demand (if applicable).

By selecting the Smart Pricing option, the Airbnb service will maximize how much you earn each night and, in some cases, increase the nightly rate on certain high-demand nights, just like traditional hotels do. For example, Airbnb may promote a lower rate for your property midweek, but charge a premium on weekend and holiday nights. Smart Pricing focuses on demand in your geographic area and automatically adjusts prices accordingly.

Keep in mind, when you turn on the Smart Pricing feature, Airbnb will never offer your property for less than what you determine is your minimum nightly rate.

After you set your nightly rate and choose between Fixed or Smart Pricing, you'll also be given the opportunity to offer a discount to guests who book and pre-pay for a full week or a full month. Offering a discount encourages longer stays. By default, Airbnb recommends offering a 21 percent discount for stays between 7 and 27 nights, and a 49 percent discount for stays longer than 28 nights. However, you are free to set your own discount rate.

aha!

Initially, you might want to avoid accepting bookings several months in advance, because between now and then, you may wind up raising your rate or altering your amenities/ offerings. Once you accept an advance reservation, the nightly rate that was quoted at the time of the booking is how much that guest will pay. You cannot change the rate after a reservation has been confirmed.

tip

For information about optional, independently operated services that can be used to automatically set and update your nightly price, based on local demand, research, and other factors, see Chapter 8, "Managing Finances for an Airbnb Hosting Business."

Step 4: Request Additional Guest Information

The Review Airbnb's Guest Requirements page gives you the opportunity to obtain additional information from prospective guests, including a confirmed email address and phone number, profile photo, and payment information. The guest will also agree to adhere to your published House Rules and share details about the purpose of their trip when requesting and booking a reservation.

If you want to gather additional information from prospective guests, click on the Add More Guest Requirements option, and then choose: Government-Issued ID Submitted to Airbnb, and/or Recommended by Other Hosts and Have No Negative Reviews.

If you live alone and are renting out a guestroom or area of your home where you'll also be staying, consider activating these additional options to help ensure your personal safety and well-being before inviting strangers to stay in your home.

From a host's standpoint, House Rules are an important aspect of a property listing. Here, you get to explain exactly what is and isn't permissible during a guest's stay. The Set House Rules for Your Guests screen offers the following options are given to you. Answer Yes or No for each:

- ▶ Suitable for Children (2–12 years)
- ▶ Suitable for Infants (Under 2 years)
- ▶ Suitable for Pets
- ▶ Smoking Allowed
- ▶ Events or Parties Allowed

There is also an Add More Rules option where you can manually add any additional rules you want to

tip

If you turn off the Instant Book feature, be prepared to respond to reservation requests as quickly as possible (within an hour or two, if possible), or you could wind up losing the booking to someone else. Furthermore, your listing will be displayed less prominently on the Airbnb website and mobile app, and according to Airbnb, "You may only get half as many reservations." You will, however, be able to block people who you're not comfortable with from staying with you, based on information within their profile and initial text message-based communications.

enforce when guests stay at your property (see the "Put Some Thought into Your House Rules" section on page 33 for more information).

If you're a new Airbnb host, consider turning off the Instant Book option on the How Guests Book screen. Simply click the Require All Guests to Send Reservation Requests op-tion. If you select the Instant Book option, you automatically accept all reservation requests immediately. By turning off this feature, you will receive a request from each prospective guest, be able to read their profile, ratings, and reviews, and then approve or deny the reservation within 24 hours of receiving the request.

Based on the available dates you've marked, the Airbnb website will ask that you confirm that what you've provided is accurate. To do this, click on the I Understand button, or click on the Go Back to Availability Settings button to tweak your property's dates of availability.

Prior to publishing your listing, select your desired Cancelation Policy. This is the policy that your guests will need to adhere to if they book a pre-paid reservation and then want or need to cancel or change that reservation. Airbnb allows you to choose between a Flexible, Moderate, Strict, Super Strict 30 Days, Super Strict 60 Days, or Long Term policy. Read the description for each

warning

As a new Airbnb host, refrain from accepting Instant Bookings. In other words, make sure the Instant Book feature remains turned off. When you turn on this feature, you allow potential guests to view your Airbnb listing and then immediately make a confirmed, pre-paid reservation, without you first having a chance to read the potential guest's profile and deny their reservation request. In other words, you'll have no say in regard to the guests who opt to stay with you. Many Airbnb hosts prefer to have the option to reject a reservation request if the potential guest has received negative reviews from past hosts, for example.

tip

At any time, to edit, change, or delete your Property Listing, sign in to the Airbnb service, click on your name/photo (displayed in the top-right corner of the browser window), and then click on the Your Listing or Dashboard option that's displayed near the top-center of the screen. Prior to publishing your listing, the message "In Progress" will appear in conjunction with your listing. When the "In Progress" message is displayed, only you can view your property listing. It is not yet public, and you cannot yet accept bookings/reservations.

▶ Create a Compelling Host Guidebook

A Host Guidebook is a section of your property listing that includes your personal suggestions when it comes to what people should see and do in the area when they visit. Your Guidebook can include local restaurants, shops, points of interest, landmarks, parks, tourist attractions, bars, or anything else nearby that you think potential guests will want to know about.

The locations for listings you add to your Host Guidebook will appear on the map that accompanies your Property Listing that shows the location of your property. To create or customize an optional Host Guidebook, sign in to your Airbnb account, click on the Manage Listings option, and then click on the Manage Listing and Calendar option. Next, click on the Guidebook option. Follow the on-screen prompts to create or edit your Host Guidebook.

Based on all of the Host Guidebooks created within your geographic area, a more general City Guidebook is also published online within the Airbnb site. This allows guests looking to stay in or near a particular area to learn more about that area prior to making their reservation.

option carefully before selecting one, because the option you choose directly determines how you'll handle guests who want to cancel or change their reservation.

Once you fine-tune each section of the Property Listing, be sure to click on the Preview button one final time to make sure all of the information is accurate, and that what you've written contains no spelling or punctuation mistakes. When you're ready, click on the Finish the Listing button to publish your listing.

Put Some Thought into Your House Rules

The House Rules you create are presented as part of your property listing, and potential guests must agree to the published rules before they can make and confirm their reservation. As a host, you'll also want to review your House Rules verbally when guests arrive at your property, and present them with a written copy of these rules upon their arrival. You'll read more on this in Chapter 5, "Responding to Broken Rules."

The goal of the House Rules is to help maintain your peace of mind as a host to ensure your guests treat your property and belongings appropriately and also act in a manner that will not bother you, other guests, or your neighbors, for example.

If guests violate your House Rules, you have the option of canceling their reservation without penalty and asking that guest to leave your premises. The Airbnb Customer Service team can help you deal with this type of situation when and if it arises.

Above and beyond the House Rules that Airbnb recommends, you can add additional rules that cater to your own wants, needs, and property. The following are a few additional House Rules you might want to implement:

- ▶ No drinking or drug use (including legalized marijuana)
- ▶ No excessive noise, loud music, or socializing between 11:00 P.M. and 7:00 A.M.
- ▶ If you allow pets, no dog walking on the front lawn
- ▶ No trespassing in the basement/attic
- ▶ No entering the host's own bedroom/bathroom
- ▶ No eating in the bedroom
- ▶ No moving or touching the artwork or antiques displayed within the property

Attracting Specific Types of Guests

Based on how you present your listing, you will be able to weed out certain types of people from requesting a reservation, and if you have the Instant Book feature turned off, you always have the option of reading a potential guest's profile, ratings, and reviews before accepting their reservation.

For example, if you do not want infants or kids staying at your property, do not promote your property as being family friendly. However, if you want short-term business professionals to stay with you, make sure you list the property as being suitable for business travelers and offer amenities that will appeal to these people.

Within your personal profile, if you enjoy quiet and solitude within your living space, mention this, but also make sure that you stipulate no groups or parties are allowed, and within your House Rules, you explain that loud noises or rowdiness is not acceptable.

aha!

In addition to house rules, consider creating a printed house manual for your property. This will be a short document that you present to your guests that offer easy-to-understand, step-by-step instructions for using the appliances in the kitchen, using the laundry facilities, where to park their car, where to find the iron and ironing board, how to use the coffee machine, how to log in to the wifi, how to turn on and use the hot tub, how to use the TV and cable box, where to find extra sheets and blankets, and how to lock/unlock the front door, for example. Based on the most commonly asked questions from your guests, you'll want to revise this house manual as needed.

Without discriminating against specific groups of people, you can describe yourself within your profile and property listing and stress that you're looking to host like-minded guests with similar interests, for example.

Offer the Best Collection of Amenities to Your Guests

Regardless of what type of property you're offering on Airbnb, it's expected to be clean, safe, and comfortable. You're also expected to provide essentials, such as clean towels, bed sheets, soap, and toilet paper, plus have one or more smoke detectors, carbon monoxide detectors, fire extinguishers, and a basic first-aid kit on hand.

However, beyond that, there are many potential amenities you can offer that will make your property that much more attractive to potential guests.

Some of the more commonly sought after amenities that potential guests will appreciate include:

- ▶ Access to a full kitchen, with a coffee maker
- ▶ Bedroom windows that open (with a view) but that have curtains or shades for privacy
- ▶ Closets with hangers and/or drawer space within a dresser
- ▶ Desk and/or workspace
- ▶ Easily accessible and available on-site or nearby parking
- ▶ Fireplace
- ▶ Fully equipped dining room (you provide dishes, silverware, glasses, etc.)
- ▶ Heat and/or air conditioning
- ▶ Hot tub/swimming pool
- ▶ In-home gym (workout equipment)
- ▶ In-home wifi
- ▶ Iron and ironing board

tip

Potential guests can search the Airbnb service for property listings based on specific amenities that are offered. By providing a broad selection of the most sought-after amenities, your listing is more apt to be noticed when it shows up based on a potential guest's personalized search parameters. This is also true with many other short-term rental services, so be sure to create and promote the most comprehensive list of amenities possible. For example, don't just say the property has a full kitchen. Describe the major appliances in that kitchen, including the microwave, coffee maker, and dishwasher, for example.

▶ Multiple power outlets and/or an available power strip within each bedroom

▶ Nightstand with reading lamp

▶ Premium bedding, blankets, and pillows (If you offer Egyptian cotton sheets with a high thread count, for example, this should be promoted within your property listing.)

▶ Secure lock on the bedroom door

▶ Shampoo, conditioner, hair dryer, and other extra toiletries in the bathroom

▶ Television with cable/satellite TV programming available

▶ Travel-size toiletries (complementary), ranging from shampoo and conditioner, to soap, mouth wash, toothpaste, etc. (These can be purchased for about $1.00 each from a dollar store, supermarket, or pharmacy.)

tip

Based on the types of guests you're looking to attract, offer bed configuration(s) that will appeal to these people. A couple will likely want a queen or king-size bed, while a solo business traveler will appreciate a queen-size bed for extra space and comfort. Friends traveling together typically prefer separate twin or queen-size beds, or two separate bedrooms. Parents traveling with kids will want one queen or king-size bed, along with a twin-size bed for each of their kids. A traditional mattress and box spring are typically preferred over a sofa bed or air mattresses, for example.

Making your property pet friendly and allowing guests to bring their pet(s) may be a sought-after amenity by some potential guests, but if there's no place for guests to walk their dog, or if you're concerned about the pets soiling your carpets, ruining your furniture, or making too much noise, think twice about allowing pets.

By offering two or more bedrooms with different bed configurations and promoting your property as "family-friendly," you're more apt to attract parents traveling with their kids. If you're looking to provide family-friendly accommodations, you may want to include a video game system, board games, and/or toys within your list of offered amenities.

Don't Forget to Protect Yourself and Your Property

As an Airbnb host, you'll ultimately be inviting strangers to stay at your property. Thus, it's in your best interest to make sure all of your belongings and furniture, for example, are properly protected. Plus, it's important that you have ample liability coverage, in case

► Meet Airbnb Superhost Mary Shimshea

Based in Allentown, Pennsylvania, Mary Shimshea is an experienced Airbnb Superhost, who owns a five-bedroom home, which she is trying to pay off using revenue she earns from Airbnb.

"I live in the home and invite guests to stay with me in my home's various bedrooms. I live near a college and a hospital, so prior to getting started with Airbnb, I was renting two of the rooms on a long-term basis to college professors. One of the professors told me about Airbnb. I visited the Airbnb website and decided it was worth a try," recalled Shimshea.

She went on to explain, "I started by doing some research in my immediate area to see how much local hotels, motels, and bed-and-breakfasts were charging. I also checked what other Airbnb hosts were charging and evaluated what they were offering for that price.

"I have always seen myself as a natural host. I like to entertain. Some of the extra things I do for my guests include providing menus for local restaurants in each of the guestrooms and displaying the clean and folded towels within nice baskets. First and foremost, I treat my guests just as I would want to be treated if I were traveling."

Prior to signing up with Airbnb, Shimshea did some research to determine local laws and tax rules that would impact her as a host. Now, after more than one year hosting with Airbnb, and offering four separate bedrooms to guests, she explains that she's been almost consistently fully booked.

"For me, being an Airbnb host has been an international experience, since I have welcomed guests from around the world. I have had so many truly nice people stay with me and try to cater to college professors, business professionals, and doctors who are traveling for work. Most of my guests want a clean and comfortable place to sleep at night, so they don't fully utilize the dining room or patio that I have set up for my guests," says Shimshea.

Because Shimshea didn't want rowdy guests staying with her, she chose her words carefully when writing her personal profile and property listing. She explains, "I use phrases like, 'cozy room with balcony,' 'serene and clean,' and 'spacious room with privacy' to describe the guestrooms.

"I also discovered that people like information about the area, so I stress that the house is located across the street from a wonderful breakfast restaurant and is a short walk away from a beautiful park. Even though I live next to a college, I have a strict policy against accepting college kids as guests. Before accepting a reservation, I always review the potential guest's

▶ Meet Airbnb Superhost, continued

profile and make sure that I'd be comfortable having that person or couple stay in my home. You can get a pretty good idea about what to expect from a guest, based on the reason they provide for their trip."

As part of her daily routine, Shimshea cleans the house and keeps it elegantly decorated. She adds, "My guests appreciate the clear effort I put into making the house as comfortable as possible for them, and as a result, I have received only five-star ratings and positive reviews. The single most sought-after amenity I offer is wifi. This is something that almost everyone requests. I also offer televisions with cable TV programming, a yard with a barbeque set up, and use of the kitchen, and I have made the house's dining room into a comfortable tea room where people can relax. I have my own pets, so I decided to accept pets and have wound up getting bookings, specifically because my home is pet friendly."

Another thing that Shimshea promotes within her listing is that she welcomes people with late arrival times when they check in. "I have had travelers show up after 10 P.M. because of travel delays, and they were very pleased that I was happy to welcome them when they arrived. I have found that travelers coming from a long distance appreciate the ability to check in late. The majority of my guests stay for one or two nights, although occasionally I welcome a guest for a full week. I had one guest stay for four months. He had a local, short-term job in the area and needed a place to stay without having to sign a one-year lease," she says.

When Shimshea first started as an Airbnb host, she purposely set her nightly rate much lower than her competition. However, as she became more experienced, she slowly increased her rates to be closer to what her competition was charging. For guests staying less than one week, she launders all of the sheets and towels, but allows her guests to launder their own clothing.

She stated, "In terms of how much interaction I have with my guests, I leave that entirely up to each guest. Some people want to go right up to their bedroom and be left alone. Others enjoy sitting with me on the porch and chatting for hours at a time. No matter what, I am always at home to welcome each guest when they first arrive. I like to be at the front door to greet each guest and to offer them a bottle of water. My guests seem to appreciate this."

Shimshea describes herself as a spiritual person who enjoys interacting with and hosting other people. However, she explains, "Being an Airbnb host is not for everyone. If you're

► **Meet Airbnb Superhost,** continued

uncomfortable with the idea of a stranger sleeping in your home, this is not something you should pursue. If you do decide to become a host, make sure you're open and honest with your prospective guests in terms of the information you provide in your profile and listing, and when you're initially communicating with people interested in staying with you. One thing I require is that people have a profile picture within their Airbnb profile."

Instead of having a front door with traditional key locks, Shimshea has a keypad that guests use to unlock the front door to enter. "Not having to distribute and then collect keys makes things a lot easier. Also, in terms of House Rules, one of the things I state is that people stay quiet after 10:00 P.M., so that everyone can get sleep and live in harmony," she says.

After welcoming each guest, Shimshea asks guests if there's anything she can do to make them more comfortable. She also encourages guests to text her if she's not available in person. "As a host, being able and willing to provide guests with information about where to go, where to eat, and what they can do during their free time is important," she adds.

"I have found that being attentive to guests definitely leads to positive ratings and reviews. For me, the biggest challenge is always being available to my guests, while also being able to enjoy my life in retirement. For me, the biggest perks of being a host are that I am continuously meeting new and interesting people and, at the same time, earning extra money while doing something that I enjoy."

someone is injured on your property. Before you begin hosting guests, be sure to speak with a licensed insurance agent in your state to determine what type of insurance and how much coverage you need.

If you plan to host families with kids or allow pets in your home, additional insurance may be required. Likewise, if you have valuable belongings, antiques, or artwork within your property, you may also need additional insurance. Determine your insurance needs, and make sure the appropriate policies are active before paying guests start staying at your property.

warning

Think twice before offering a crib or specialized gear for infants/toddlers within your property, or you could be held accountable if, for whatever reason, the infant or young child is injured using that crib or child-specific furniture. Instead, promote that the bedroom has ample space for parents to bring and set up their own pack-and-play crib, for example.

Creating an attention-getting personal profile and property listing on Airbnb is your first big step toward becoming a successful and money-earning host. It's also necessary, however, to properly set up and prepare your property for guests. How to do this is the focus of the next chapter.

How to Use the Airbnb Website and Mobile App

Airbnb is an online community and service that's based on the internet. It's available 24-hours-per-day, seven-days-per-week, from any computer or mobile device that connects to the internet.

To access Airbnb from your internet-connected computer, use your favorite web browser—such as Microsoft Edge (Windows PC), Safari (Mac), Google Chrome (PC/Mac),

Foxfire (PC/Mac), Opera (PC/Mac), or Internet Explorer (if you're using an older Windows PC that is not running the Windows 10 operating system)—and visit www.airbnb.com.

What makes using Airbnb incredibly convenient for you as a host is that virtually all of the same tools that are available from your computer are also available using the Airbnb mobile app from your internet-connected iPhone, iPad, or any Android-based smartphone or tablet. These tools include the ability to manage your account, create or edit your personal profile, create or manage your property listings, manage bookings, and interact with (potential) guests.

This means that you don't need to sit in front of a computer to manage online tasks associated with being an Airbnb host. These tasks can be handled from virtually anywhere. Thus, to be a truly efficient Airbnb host, you'll probably want to invest in a smartphone or tablet.

A smartphone can use a 3G/4G/LTE cellular data connection (which you pay for through your cellular service provider) or wifi to connect to the internet and allow the phone to access Airbnb's service via its mobile app. However, if you opt to use a tablet, such as an iPad, based on your lifestyle and where you'll be using it, you can choose between a wifi-only tablet, or a slightly more expensive tablet with wifi plus cellular internet connectivity.

> ▶ A wifi-only tablet allows you to connect to the internet (and use the Airbnb mobile app) anytime the device is connected to a wifi hotspot, which could be from your home, at work, at school, at a public library, at an internet café or coffee shop, at a hotel, or at any airport, for example. However, if you're driving around in your car, or not within the signal radius of a wifi hotspot, the wifi-only tablet will not be able to connect to the internet. Thus, the Airbnb mobile app won't fully function.
>
> ▶ A wifi-plus-cellular tablet can keep you connected to the internet when you're within the signal radius of a wifi hotspot. However, if no wifi

tip

When relying on your mobile device to manage your Airbnb account, you don't need to keep the Airbnb mobile app continuously running on your smartphone or tablet. Instead, simply set up the Notifications and Alerts options (which on an iPhone/iPad is done from the Notifications menu within Settings, not from the Airbnb app itself). Your smartphone/tablet will automatically receive a text message (or your smartphone or tablet will automatically receive a Push Notification) anytime a (potential) guest sends you a message, you receive a new booking, or something related to your Airbnb account needs your attention.

hotspot is available, it allows you to connect to the internet using a 3G/4G/LTE cellular data connection, which is available almost anywhere in the country (indoors or outdoors). This option gives you more flexibility in terms of when and where you can use the Airbnb mobile app. Because you're using a tablet, you can view more content on the tablet's screen, versus using the smartphone edition of the app.

Remember, whether you're using a computer or mobile device to manage your Airbnb account and to handle all of the administrative hosting tasks related to the service (including managing reservations and communicating with guests via Airbnb's messaging service), you'll need to have a continuous internet connection. The good news is that you do not need the latest model computer, smartphone, or tablet to access the Airbnb service, as long as the equipment you use is capable of connecting to the internet and running a web browser (for computer users) or running the Airbnb mobile app (for smartphone and tablet users).

While the focus of this book is on how to be a successful Airbnb host, virtually all of the other short-term rental services that are online-based operate in much the same way as Airbnb. So, once you become familiar with how to create and manage an Airbnb account as a host, you should have little trouble adapting these skills if you opt to work with a competing service.

In addition, many of the other short-term rental services that were discussed in Chapter 1, "Changing the Way People Travel," and that you'll learn more about from Chapter 9, "Other Related Services You Should Be Aware Of," also have a proprietary mobile app you can use to manage your account with that service. You'll find these apps available from the App Store (iPhone/iPad) or Google Play Store (Android).

Get Acquainted with Using the Airbnb Website

Virtually everything you'll be doing online related to your responsibilities as an Airbnb host can be handled directly from the Airbnb website (www.airbnb.com). Once you have bookings and you're in contact with your guests, some of this communication can also be done via email or through social media (Facebook, Twitter, LinkedIn, or Snapchat, for example). However, for your own security, it's best to communicate with your potential guests and booked guests as much as possible through the Airbnb

aha!

If your web browser is set up to remember your website-specific usernames and passwords and sign you into each website upon a return visit, each time you revisit the Airbnb.com website, your name will be displayed in the top-right corner of the browser window, instead of the Sign In option.

messaging service, because a detailed transcript of all that transpires is maintained by Airbnb.

As you learned from Chapter 2, "Get Started as an Airbnb Host," one of the first things you'll need to do once you opt to become an Airbnb host (or use the Airbnb service as a guest) is create a personal Airbnb account. This can be done from the Airbnb website or mobile app.

Then, to proceed with becoming an Airbnb host, you'll need to create one or more property listings, which can also be done from the Airbnb website or mobile app, although it's more convenient to do this from a computer with a larger screen. How to set yourself up as an Airbnb host is also covered within Chapter 2.

Once your personal account and property listing(s) are created, everything having to do with managing your account and listings, as well as virtually all administrative tasks associated with being a host, can be handled from the Airbnb website. So, it's important that you become familiar with what's possible from the website and develop a basic understanding of how to navigate around the site.

Depending on whether you have your computer's web browser set up to remember your website-specific usernames and passwords, it may or may not be necessary to sign into the Airbnb website each time you access it. If after you've set up your Airbnb account you're required to sign in during subsequent visits, click on the Log In option that's displayed in the top-right corner of the browser window once the Airbnb homepage has loaded.

> **warning**
>
> As an Airbnb host, if you have a desktop computer set up in your property that your guests will have access to, do not allow the computer to remember your usernames or passwords. You do not want one of your guests being able to hack into your Airbnb account and take control over it. For your own security, make sure you keep your Airbnb account password private at all times and in a secure place your guests cannot access. Obviously, this security precaution applies to all of your usernames and passwords for your online banking, investment, online shopping, and credit card management accounts, for example.

Handling Hosting-Related Administrative Tasks from the Airbnb Website

Once you've signed into the Airbnb website, and you have set yourself up as a host (by following the directions outlined in Chapter 2), it's possible to handle all online-based administrative tasks associated with being an Airbnb host.

The Airbnb website is continuously evolving. New features and functions are always being added, and the design and user interface of the website is periodically tweaked. As a result, your navigation experience when you access some of the features and functions outlined in this chapter may be different.

At any time, if you have a question about using a specific website feature or function, simply click on the Help option that's displayed near the top-right corner of the Airbnb.com web browser window, and then within the Search field, type a keyword, question, or search phrase that relates to what you need help with. You will discover, however, that the overall design and user interface that's associated with the Airbnb.com website is well-designed, intuitive, and easy to navigate.

Figure 3.1 offers a rundown of some common administrative tasks for hosts featured on Airbnb.

Airbnb.com Commonly Used Hosting Features

Administrative Airbnb Hosting Task	What It's Used For	How to Access It
Edit Your Personal Profile	Add or change personal information included in your Airbnb personal profile. This includes adding photos and/or videos, completing the Verified ID process, as well as managing your reviews and references.	Click on your username or profile photo thumbnail that's displayed in the top-right corner of the browser window, and then select the Edit Profile option from the menu that's displayed.
Refer Your Friends to Airbnb	When you invite your friends (via email or social media) to join Airbnb as a host or guest, you get rewarded. Use these tools to manage your invites.	Click on your username or profile photo thumbnail that's displayed in the top-right corner of the browser window, and then select the Referrals option from the menu that's displayed.
Adjust Account Settings	Add or edit details in your Airbnb account, including payment methods, payout preferences, your transaction history, privacy options, security options, linking your Airbnb mobile app to your account, adjusting account-specific settings, and promoting yourself online with Airbnb Badges.	Click on your username or profile photo thumbnail that's displayed in the top-right corner of the browser window, and then select the Account Settings option from the menu that's displayed. A separate Account Settings menu screen is displayed. Use the menu options displayed on the left to access each submenu, and adjust settings for individual options.

FIGURE 3–1: **Airbnb.com Commonly Used Hosting Features**

Airbnb.com Commonly Used Hosting Features

Administrative Airbnb Hosting Task	What It's Used For	How to Access It
Learn About Airbnb for Business	Determine if you want to apply to become an Airbnb for Business host, and learn more about this aspect of the service that caters to business travelers.	Click on your username or profile photo thumbnail that's displayed in the top-right corner of the browser window, and then select the Business Travel option from the menu that's displayed.
Access and Manage City Guidebooks	Access city- or region-specific Guidebooks that share information about local businesses, restaurants, tourist attractions, points of interest, or landmarks that your guests might be interested in.	Click on your username or profile photo thumbnail that's displayed in the top-right corner of the browser window, and then select the My Guidebooks option from the menu that's displayed.
Log Out from the Airbnb Website	Prevent an unauthorized person from using your computer to log in to your Airbnb account as you.	When you're done using the Airbnb website, be sure to sign out from the service instead of just closing the web browser. Click on your username or profile photo thumbnail that's displayed in the top-right corner of the browser window, and then select the Log Out option from the menu that's displayed.
Communicate with (Potential) Guests Using the Airbnb Messaging Service	As you learned from the previous chapter, communication between (potential) and confirmed guests is done via Airbnb's secure text messaging service. Use this tool to respond to incoming messages, or refer back to past conversations, for example.	Click on the Messages option that's displayed near the top-right corner of the browser window, and then select either the View Inbox or View Dashboard option. View Inbox allows you to see and respond to newly received messages. View Dashboard allows you to manage all past conversations as a host or guest, based on how you've used the Airbnb service in the past.

FIGURE 3–1: **Airbnb.com Commonly Used Hosting Features,** continued

Airbnb.com Commonly Used Hosting Features

Administrative Airbnb Hosting Task	What It's Used For	How to Access It
Access the Host Dashboard	The Dashboard is a central hub or control center to quickly see what tasks related to your Airbnb account need your attention. For example, you might need to complete an unfinished property listing, have inbox messages to respond to, or address alerts that have been sent to you from Airbnb.	Click on the Host option that's displayed near the top-right corner of the browser window, and then select the Dashboard option.
Manage Your Property Listing(s)	Add, update, or edit a property listing. This includes being able to alter your Nightly Rate, Availability, and Booking-related settings that were discussed within Chapter 2.	Click on the Host option that's displayed near the top-right corner of the browser window, and then select the Manage Listings option. Select which listing you want to manage, and then click on the Start with the Basics, Set the Scene, or Get Ready for Guests option in order to access the related submenus. Alternatively, after clicking on the Manage Listing option, click on the Your Listing, Your Reservations, Reservation Requirements, or Add New Listing option, which are displayed toward the left side of the browser window.
Create a New Property Listing	If you're offering multiple rooms within a single property, or two or more separate properties as an Airbnb host, you will need to create a separate property listing for each.	Click on the Host option that's displayed near the top-right corner of the browser window, and then select the List Your Space option. Click on Step 1, Step 2, and then Step 3, and complete the online questionnaire. Refer back to Chapter 2 for details.

FIGURE 3–1: **Airbnb.com Commonly Used Hosting Features,** continued

Airbnb.com Commonly Used Hosting Features

Administrative Airbnb Hosting Task	What It's Used For	How to Access It
Access and Manage Reservations (Bookings)	Once guests start booking your property through Airbnb, manage these reservations online using the hosting tools provided.	Click on the Host option that's displayed near the top-right corner of the browser window, and then select the Your Reservations option. Each reservation will be listed separately. Click on the one you want to review or manage.
Access Your Transaction History	Airbnb handles all financial transactions for you. To see a detailed accounting of all current, future, and pending financial transactions, use these hosting tools.	Click on the Host option that's displayed near the top-right corner of the browser window, and then select the Transactions History option. Click on any of the menu options displayed on the left side of the screen to handle various aspects of financial account settings, such as Payout Preferences or Payment Methods.
Access Your Reviews	Airbnb hosts succeed or fail based on their reviews. Plus, as a host, you're able to write reviews for each of your guests after they've stayed with you. Use these tools to view and manage all functionality related to viewing or composing reviews.	Click on the Host option that's displayed near the top-right corner of the browser window, and then select the Reviews option. Next, click on the Reviews About You tab to read reviews your guests have written about you, or click on the Reviews By You tab to access tools for reading reviews you've written and composing reviews. Remember, once a review is published, it typically can't be deleted or edited. A response from the person who was reviewed, however, can be published and displayed in conjunction with the actual review.
Learn About Host Assist Services	Airbnb has teamed up with a handful of companies that offer products or services that are potentially beneficial to Airbnb hosts, such as home security systems and keyless entry door locks. Learn more about what's offered by accessing this area of the Airbnb website.	Click on the Host option that's displayed near the top-right corner of the browser window, and then select the Host Assist option. Click on one of the companies that are listed, or click on the pull-down menu that's displayed near the top-center of the browser window in order to sort the companies and services by category.

FIGURE 3–1: **Airbnb.com Commonly Used Hosting Features,** continued

Airbnb.com Commonly Used Hosting Features

Administrative Airbnb Hosting Task	What It's Used For	How to Access It
Master Your Hospitality Skills	Read tips and strategies from Airbnb about how to enhance your hospitality skills and become a better host.	Click on the Host option that's displayed near the top-right corner of the browser window, and then select the Hospitality option. From this web page, click on one of the command tabs that are displayed near the top-center of the browser window, which include: About, Availability, Communication, Commitment, Check-In, Accuracy, Cleanliness, and Overall Experience.
Get Online Help	Airbnb has set up a massive, interactive database to help you get answers to virtually any question you have about the Airbnb service, plus learn how to use every feature and function the website or mobile app offers.	Click on the Help option that's displayed near the top-center of the browser window, and then fill in the What Can We Help You With? field that's displayed. It's also possible to click on a link to read a recommended article that's displayed, or click on the Help Center option in order to access a more interactive help feature.
Contact Airbnb	Receive assistance from Airbnb's Customer Service department.	To contact Airbnb's online customer service department, visit www.airbnb.com/help/contact_us. To send or request money via the Airbnb service, utilize the Resolution Center by visiting: www.airbnb.com/resolution_center. You also have the option of calling Airbnb's Customer Service department at (855) 424-7262 or (415) 800-5959.
Return to the Airbnb Home Page	Regardless of what you're doing within the Airbnb.com website, you can always return to the website's homepage.	Click on the Airbnb logo that's displayed near the top-left corner of the browser window.

FIGURE 3–1: **Airbnb.com Commonly Used Hosting Features,** continued

Airbnb.com Commonly Used Hosting Features

Administrative Airbnb Hosting Task	What It's Used For	How to Access It
Quickly Adjust the Instant Book Settings	Once your host account is active you're able to quickly turn on or off the Instant Book setting. When turned on, any guest can book and confirm a reservation to stay at your property. You forfeit the opportunity to review the potential guest's request and profile before approving the booking.	From the Airbnb home page (or almost any page within the website) scroll to the very bottom of the browser window, and click on the Instant Book option that's displayed below the Hosting heading.
Learn More About Home Safety	As a host, it's your responsibility to offer a clean, comfortable, and safe place for your guests to stay. Access tips and important information related to making your property safe for guests.	From the Airbnb home page (or almost any page within the website) scroll to the very bottom of the browser window, and click on the Home Safety option that's displayed below the Hosting heading.
Cancel (Close) Your Airbnb Account or Hide Your Listing	Close your Airbnb account and erase all personal information about you and your property from the Airbnb service, or temporarily hide your property listing(s) from the public.	Click on your username or profile photo thumbnail that's displayed in the top-right corner of the browser window, and then select the Account Settings option from the menu that's displayed. Next, click on the Settings option from the menu that's displayed on the left side of the screen, and click on the Cancel My Account button. Provide the reason you want to cancel, and then click on the Cancel My Account button again to finalize your decision. (This cannot be undone.) Alternatively, you can use the Hide My Listing feature to keep your account and property listing from being seen by others, until you're ready to become active on the service again. For information on how to do this, visit: www.airbnb.com/help/article/476/how-do-i-snooze-or-deactivate-my-listing.

FIGURE 3–1: **Airbnb.com Commonly Used Hosting Features,** continued

Keep in mind, as you navigate around the Airbnb website, there are often multiple ways to access commonly used features and functions. For example, hyperlinks or buttons that will help you navigate are often located near the top-center of the browser window or are embedded in the contents of specific Airbnb web pages.

How to Set Your Payout Preferences with Airbnb

As an Airbnb host, chances are you want to be paid in a timely, accurate, and convenient manner. Well, all money that exchanges between Airbnb hosts and guests happens via the

▶ Refer Your Family and Friends to Airbnb and Get Rewarded

If you're like most people, you've probably created an extensive database of personal and professional contacts (including friends, family members, and coworkers) on your PC or Mac. Perhaps you're also active on social media services like Facebook, Instagram, Twitter, Snapchat, or LinkedIn.

Airbnb will reward you for reaching out to your friends, family, and coworkers, as well as your online network, and provides the tools for doing this. For example, after referring someone to Airbnb, if he or she sets up a free account and then stays with any Airbnb host as a guest, you receive a $35 travel credit. However, if the person you refer becomes an Airbnb host, you receive a $75 travel credit when he or she welcomes their first guest.

You can read more about the terms and conditions associated with the Airbnb Referral program by visiting www.airbnb.com/referrals/terms_and_conditions. If you're comfortable inviting people to become part of the Airbnb community, the Airbnb website gives you the tools to quickly email people within your email address database or share an invitation via your social media accounts and/or Facebook Messenger. To do this, visit: www.airbnb.com/invite.

While there is the financial upside for you and the friends you invite using these tools, anyone you invite will receive an unsolicited email message, text message, or message via social media, that comes from you on behalf of Airbnb. It's entirely your decision about whether or not you want to share information about your contacts with Airbnb in order to take advantage of the Referral Rewards program.

Keep in mind, you can discuss the opportunity with specific friends or relatives in person or on the phone, and then use Airbnb's tools to send invites only to those people who are interested.

Airbnb website. This provides one centralized place where all Airbnb-related financial transactions are handled, which makes bookkeeping that much easier for hosts like you.

Before welcoming your first guest as an Airbnb host, it's important that you provide Airbnb with the appropriate financial information that's needed for you to make payments, as well as receive payments, through the service. It's then your responsibility to keep this information up to date, if your bank account details change, for example.

To set up Airbnb's Payment Methods and Payout Preferences from your computer, follow these steps:

1. Go to www.airbnb.com and sign into your Airbnb account.
2. Click on your username or profile photo thumbnail that's displayed in the top-right corner of the web browser window.
3. From the menu that appears, click on the Account Settings option.
4. Click on the Payment Methods option, and then click on the Add Payment Method option. (This is required if you're an Airbnb host, or a guest, as the payment method(s) you add will be used to make payments to other hosts when you travel, or potentially to issue refunds to your guests.)
5. An Add New Payment Method window will appear with Visa, MasterCard, American Express, and Discover card logos displayed at the top of this window.
6. Enter your Card Number, Card Expiration Date, Card Security Code, First Name, Last Name, Postal Code, and Country.
7. Click on the Add Card button to continue. After completing the payment method section, details about that credit or debit card will be displayed under the Payment Methods heading. You can then add an additional credit or debit card to the

warning

As an Airbnb income-earning host, you will need to pay taxes. This is not something that Airbnb handles on your behalf. It is your responsibility, based on the location of your property and where you live, to determine what taxes you're responsible for, what tax forms need to be completed and submitted, and to make sure your tax debt is paid on time. Failure to pay all of the proper local, state, and federal taxes will result in high fines from the government, and could easily lead to other legal problems. It's a really good strategy to consult with an accountant who is familiar with short-term rentals, and to seek help setting up or handling your bookkeeping and tax-related paperwork, so that tax payments are paid correctly.

account, if you wish, and then choose which card you want to be your default card when making payments through Airbnb.

8. Once you've added one or more payment methods to your Airbnb account, click on the Payout Preferences option. You must set up a payout method in order to be paid by Airbnb for your hosting service or to receive payments from guests. Keep in mind, Airbnb transfers the funds that are owed to you approximately 24 hours after a guest's scheduled check-in time. It then takes time for the funds to appear in your account. How much time it takes to actually receive your money will be based on the payout method you select, as well as your bank or financial institution.

9. Click the Payout Methods option, and then click on the Add Payout Method button to set this up.

10. You will be asked to provide your complete address. Fill in the appropriate fields, and click on the Next button.

11. Select one of the following three payout options, and then click on the Next button:

   ▶ *Direct Deposit (ACH).* This takes up to three business days for funds to appear within your account; however, there are no additional fees. This method works only on business days, so no transactions take place on weekends or bank holidays. If you choose this method, you will be prompted to enter the name on the bank account, select the type of account it is (checking or savings), and then provide the bank's routing number and your unique account number. This is information displayed in the lower-left corner of your printed checks, or it can be obtained from your bank. Click the Finish button after entering this information.

   ▶ *PayPal.* This option takes just a few hours to process and receive your funds, but you first need to set up a separate PayPal account (www.paypal.com). If you opt to transfer funds out of your PayPal account once they're received, however, you will have to pay PayPal withdrawal fees.

   ▶ *Payoneer Prepaid Debit MasterCard.* If you choose this option, you will be mailed a physical prepaid debit card in the mail. Money you earn from Airbnb will be transferred to this prepaid account and can be spent using the prepaid MasterCard you receive. However, if you use this card at an ATM to withdraw cash, ATM withdrawal fees will apply. It only takes a few hours for Airbnb to transfer funds to you using this method. To set up this Payoneer Prepaid Debit MasterCard account, the Airbnb website will transfer you to a separate website, which will request your name, address, and other relevant information. For more information about the fees associated with this option, visit: www.payoneer.com/fees.

▶ Avoid Linking Your Debit Card with Your Airbnb Account

Don't link a debit card to your Airbnb account. Just as when making any type of online purchases, refrain from using your debit card for anything online. Instead, use a major credit card, if possible.

When you use a debit card for online financial transactions, the money is immediately removed from the bank account that the card is linked to, and the merchant is paid. If you later wind up having a problem with your purchase or the merchant, you will need to turn to your bank for assistance, and the protection you receive will be limited. For example, if you're a victim of debit card or online fraud, it could take weeks or months to recover your money.

However, by using a major credit card for all online purchases, for example, you automatically receive a much higher level of protection. If you have trouble with the merchant or with a purchase, you simply need to contact your credit card issuer to process a dispute or request a chargeback.

In addition, by linking a major credit card with your Airbnb account, if an unauthorized person gains access to your Airbnb account, they won't have direct access to your debit card details, and thus your bank account information, which keeps you better protected.

All financial information you provide to Airbnb will be kept confidential, however, you must not allow unauthorized people to gain access to your Airbnb account. Be sure to keep your login information private.

Once you've set up your Airbnb Payout Preferences and begin earning money, you can access your Transaction History at any time. This is information you'll need to keep track of your personal finances and income, as well as when it comes to tax return preparation and filing.

Additional information about managing your finances as an Airbnb host is provided in Chapter 8, "Managing Finances for an Airbnb Hosting Business."

Discover How to Use the Airbnb iPhone/iPad App

The Airbnb mobile app for the Apple iPhone or iPad can be used to handle almost all of the same tasks as you'd otherwise handle from the Airbnb website.

To download and install the Airbnb mobile app, follow these steps:

1. Launch the App Store app from the Home screen on your iPhone or iPad.
2. On an iPhone, tap on the Search icon at the bottom of the screen, or on the iPad, tap on the Featured icon, and then tap on the Search field that's displayed in the top-right corner of the tablet's screen.
3. Within the Search field, type "Airbnb," and when the search results are displayed, tap on the Get button that's associated with the Airbnb app listing (from Airbnb, Inc.). Follow the same process as you normally would to download and install a new app onto your mobile device.
4. Once the app is installed, the Airbnb app icon will be displayed on your iPhone or iPad's Home screen. Tap on the app icon to launch the app.
5. From the opening screen, tap on the Log In option to sign in to your Airbnb account.
6. When prompted, enter your Airbnb account username and password, and then tap on the Yes, Notify Me button when the Turn On Notifications? option is displayed. The Airbnb mobile app will go online, access the Airbnb service, and allow you to manage all aspects of your account as long as your iPhone or iPad maintains its internet connection. From left to right, the following five command icons are displayed along the bottom of the screen:

   ▶ *Airbnb Logo.* Tap on this icon to access the Airbnb Home screen.
   ▶ *Search.* Tap on this icon as a guest to find an Airbnb property to stay at during your next trip.
   ▶ *Messages.* Tap on this icon to launch Airbnb's text messaging service, access your inbox, and communicate with your (potential) guests, or your host if you're the

▶ How to Create and Display Airbnb Badges Online

If you maintain your own web page or blog, for example, Airbnb has made it easy for you to display a graphic Airbnb badge that invites people to see your Airbnb profile and/or view your property listing.

Upon selecting a badge style and answering a few online questions, you'll be provided with HTML code that can be cut and pasted into your website or blog, so that the Airbnb badge is displayed and becomes interactive. For more information about this feature, visit: www.airbnb.com/users/badges.

one who will be doing the traveling. Each of your message threads will be displayed separately, so you can quickly switch between conversations by tapping on the appropriate message thread listing.

▶ *Trips.* Tap on this icon to view details about your past, present, or future trips as a guest (traveler) using the Airbnb service.

▶ *Profile.* Tap on this icon to access a menu that provides you with options for managing your account profile, adjusting your account settings, accessing help and support, creating a listing, accessing the hosting features, providing feedback to Airbnb, or referring friends to Airbnb.

Manage Host-Related Tasks from the Airbnb Mobile App

As a host, after tapping on the Profile icon, tap on the Switch to Hosting menu option in order to access a complete selection of tools used to manage your bookings, property listing(s), and the administrative tasks associated with being an Airbnb host.

A new set of command icons will be displayed along the bottom of the screen. From left to right, these include the Reservation Management icon, Your Listing icon, Your Calendar icon, the Host Dashboard icon, and the Profile icon.

Tap on the Pending icon to manage reservation requests and booking inquiries from potential guests. It's from here you can accept or reject a booking or check out a prospective guest's profile.

Tap on the Your Listing icon to edit any aspect of your property listing(s), or tap on the Add New Listing button to create a new property listing from scratch. Although you're handling these tasks from a mobile device, the process is basically the same as when using the Airbnb website.

Tap on the Your Calendar icon to manage your property's availability and adjust the Calendar Settings, such as Advance Notice, Preparation Time, Distant Requests, and Minimum/Maximum Stay. These options work the same was as they do on the Airbnb website, but they can be adjusted or managed from your smartphone or tablet.

Tap on the Host Dashboard icon to access an at-a-glance overview of your property listings, earnings, and hosting activities. While the location on the screen of dashboard-related information is different from the Airbnb website, the information provided in the mobile app is basically the same.

Tap on the Profile icon to manage all aspects of your Airbnb profile. From this menu, tap on the Switch to Traveling option to switch from the hosting tools to the main Airbnb traveling/guest toolset.

► Get Social with Airbnb

Airbnb's official Facebook page allows employees to interact with its community members and allows hosts to communicate informally among themselves. To "Like" this page and become active on it, you must have an established Facebook account, which you can set up for free by visiting www.facebook.com, filling in the prompts displayed below the Sign Up heading, and then clicking on the Sign Up button, or by using the official Facebook app on your mobile device.

Once you're active on Facebook, visit www.facebook.com/airbnb to access Airbnb's official Facebook page, and click on the "Like" button that's associated with the page to join it. From the Facebook page, you can participate on the message board, view photos and videos, plus learn about upcoming events, for example.

Airbnb is also active on YouTube (www.youtube.com/user/Airbnb), Twitter (@airbnb or @airbnbhelp), Instagram (www.instagram.com/airbnb), Google+ (https://plus.google.com/+airbnb), and LinkedIn (www.linkedin.com/company/airbnb).

If you have an urgent question, one way to reach Airbnb directly is via Twitter, using the @airbnbhelp username when posting a tweet that contains your question. This is a public forum, so be careful about posting any personal information within the message.

Airbnb also hosts an interactive, online forum called the Airbnb Community Center that allows hosts to freely communicate with one another in order to share stories, tips, and ideas. Participation is free. To get involved, visit: https://community.airbnb.com/t5/Community-Center/ct-p/community-center.

Yet another way to interact with fellow Airbnb hosts in your city is to participate in an in-person Airbnb Meet Up. These are informal gatherings that are scheduled throughout the world by Airbnb hosts. For more information about how to participate, visit: www.airbnb.com/meetups.

Manage All Aspects of Your Airbnb Account from an Android Smartphone or Tablet

The official Airbnb mobile app for Android smartphones and tablets works very much the same as the iPhone/iPad app. However, this version of the app is available for free from the Google Play Store.

To download and install the app follow these steps:

1. Launch the Play Store app from your Android mobile device.

2. Once your mobile device connects to the Google Play Store, within the Search field that's displayed near the top of the screen, enter the keyword "Airbnb," and then tap on the Search key.

3. The official Airbnb mobile app (from Airbnb, Inc.) should be displayed as the first search result. Tap on the search result listing to reveal details about the app. Next, tap on the Install button to download and install the free Airbnb mobile app onto your Android smartphone or tablet.

4. Tap on the Airbnb app icon to launch the app. The Welcome to Airbnb screen is displayed. Tap on the Log In option to log in to your existing Airbnb account using your username and password. You can also choose to Continue with Facebook, or tap on the Create Account button to create a new Airbnb account from scratch.

5. After you've logged in to your Airbnb account from the mobile app, you'll be able to use the Smart Lock feature to remember your username and password, so you will be automatically signed in anytime you relaunch the Airbnb mobile app.

6. The main Airbnb home screen is displayed next. The information on this screen is virtually identical to what you'd find on Airbnb's website home screen. To access the various features and functions offered by the app, tap on the Menu icon that's displayed in the top-left corner of the screen.

7. The initial menu offers more than a dozen options for managing your Airbnb account and the guest aspects of the account. Tap the Switch to Hosting option when you need to access the hosting tools.

You can manage your reservation requests from your Android mobile device. Tap on the Menu icon that's displayed in the top-left corner of the screen to access each of the hosting tools. Options include: Host Home, Calendar, Listings, Performance, Inbox, Profile, List Your Space, Invite Friends, Help, Give Us Feedback, and Switch to Traveling.

As you'll discover, all of the same hosting tools that are available on the Airbnb website are also available via the mobile app. Thus, you can handle the majority of your Airbnb hosting administrative tasks from almost anywhere, as long as your smartphone or tablet has access to the internet.

Preparing Your Property

Regardless of the service you choose, before accepting your first booking as a host, it's necessary to prepare every aspect of your property for guests. In order to provide a clean, comfortable, efficient, visually pleasing, and safe environment, some of the things you'll probably need to do include:

- ▶ Rearrange some of your existing furniture to make the living space more accessible and comfortable for guests
- ▶ Remove clutter and personal items from where your guests will be staying
- ▶ Remove political and/or religious décor or paraphernalia from where your guests will be staying
- ▶ Fine tune the overall décor
- ▶ Ensure that the living space is safe for guests
- ▶ Install proper indoor and outdoor lighting and safety equipment as needed
- ▶ Invest in the purchase of furniture, beds, bedding, towels, and amenities to be used by your guests
- ▶ Thoroughly clean the property, and hire an optional professional cleaning/maid service you'll use on an ongoing basis
- ▶ Make sure all your appliances, home electronics, wifi, and other equipment are fully functional
- ▶ Have copies of front door keys made, or install smart door locks with programmable keypads so guests can easily come and go as they please using a numeric code that you provide
- ▶ Write a house manual for your guests
- ▶ Collect menus from nearby restaurants (and determine which restaurants deliver, as well as their delivery hours), as well as brochures from nearby attractions and points of interest to have on hand for your guests

To accomplish some of these tasks, chances are you'll need to make an upfront financial investment, which hopefully you'll quickly recoup once you start having paid guests stay at your property. Another approach is to handle the most important tasks first, initially charge a lower nightly rate, and then use your profits from paying guests to improve the property over time. Then, as the living space becomes more comfortable and luxurious, you can begin charging a higher nightly rate.

Think Safety First

In addition to acquiring all of the necessary insurance, make sure your property provides the safest living space possible. Be sure to install and test the smoke detectors, carbon monoxide detectors, fire extinguishers, flashlights, and a first-aid kit, for example. Also, check every piece of furniture to make sure it's working properly, sturdy, and safe (for adults and kids alike) for use.

Some of the additional safety-oriented measures you should take care of include:

▶ If you have a large bookcase or display cabinet, make sure it's securely bolted to the wall and can't accidently fall on and injure someone.

▶ If you're allowing guests to use your kitchen appliances and/or laundry facilities, make sure the equipment is functioning properly and clean.

▶ Check all of the electrical wiring in your home, and make sure it's up to date with building codes and that you don't have any unsafe extension cords or wires on the floors or walls that guests can trip over or get themselves caught on. This is particularly important if you'll be allowing families with young kids or pets to stay at your property.

▶ Make sure your flat screen television is securely bolted to the wall or mounted on a stand that can't accidently get knocked over.

▶ Install nonslip mats on the floor of each shower and/or bathtub.

▶ Install or make sure all lighting in the exterior of your home works, and consider adding an automatic timer, so the parking area/driveway and main entrance to your property is well lit from sundown to sunrise.

▶ Ensure that all of the interior lighting fixtures and lamps are functioning properly, are sturdy, provide ample lighting, and are easily accessible. Also keep a supply of extra light bulbs on hand.

▶ Install separate door locks (which lock from the inside) on each guestroom door, so guests will feel safer at night while they're sleeping.

Decorating and Furnishing Your Property

When it comes to decorating and furnishing your home, think in terms of efficiency, functionality, durability, comfort, and appearance. There are several directions you can go. Either offer low-end furniture that's durable and charge a lower nightly rate, or go all out and offer high-quality furnishings and décor that will allow you to charge a premium nightly rate, for example.

If you go with the economical and affordable approach, furnish your guestroom(s) like you'd furnish a college dormitory, with basic, low-cost, but highly durable

tip

Be sure to leave open space within each guestroom, especially if it's a small space. Remember, people will have luggage with them and will need to place their suitcases where they're easily accessible. Consider adding a luggage rack in each guestroom for the added convenience of your guests and so they don't accidently ruin or scratch the furniture, for example, by piling their suitcase on top of it.

furnishings that include a bed, nightstand, dresser, mirror, trashcan, lamp(s), nightstand light, and possibly a desk and deckchair. Functionality takes precedence over appearance and luxury, but you should still offer clean and comfortable accommodations.

Keep in mind that most people travel with a notebook computer, tablet, smartphone, ebook reader, digital camera, and/or other consumer electronics that need to be plugged in. Whenever possible, offer multiple, easily accessible electrical outlets in each bedroom, or include an extension cord and a multi-outlet power strip within each guestroom.

By taking the economical approach, you can do your furniture shopping at Ikea (www.ikea.com), or another low-cost furniture store, decorate the guestroom walls with one or two posters or pieces of generic (non-offensive) artwork, and offer decent, but inexpensive bedding (sheets, blankets, pillows, etc.) that you purchase from Ikea, Target, Walmart, or Bed, Bath & Beyond, for example.

As for the kitchen and dining room area, if you take an economical approach, consider offering plastic dishes, silverware, and cups that won't break and that are easily washable or disposable. Provide paper towels and paper napkins that can be thrown away after use (as opposed to dish towels or cloth napkins that need to be laundered). In the bathroom, offer clean towels, and bathroom mats, plus always put extra emphasis on the cleanliness of the bathroom itself. Your guests should never see mold, mildew, soap scum, or dirt anywhere in the bathroom (including on the floor, as well as in and around the sink, toilet, shower/ bathtub, or on the shower curtain).

The Furnishing, Décor, and Amenities You Provide Can Impact Your Nighty Rate

If you opt for a higher-end approach to your furnishings and décor to provide a more comfortable and luxurious living space for your guests, you should definitely promote this approach within your Airbnb property listing, and it should be reflected in your nightly rate. People will pay more for luxury and added comfort. (This applies to hosting with all short-term rental services, not just Airbnb.)

tip

If you target a really high-end clientele by offering a property in the middle of an upscale community or neighborhood and you'll be charging a premium, consider hiring a professional interior decorator to decorate the property, especially the bedrooms. Again, focus on comfort, efficiency, safety, and cleanliness, in addition to appearance.

When you opt to take this approach, the expectations of your guests will be much higher. The upfront cost to decorate and furnish each guestroom or your property will also be higher, but you should easily be able to recuperate the additional costs by charging a higher nightly rate.

By targeting a higher-paying clientele, understand that they'll expect nicer furniture, more luxurious bed linens, pillows, and blankets and more elegant artwork and décor, plus fancier and brand-name amenities. These people will be harder to please and potentially less apt to write unsolicited reviews (unless they're very disappointed with their experience staying at your property).

On the plus side, if you have a flare for interior decorating and hospitality, you can do more, be more creative, and showcase some of your personal taste with your selection of furniture, décor, and artwork, for example. You can also include extra amenities like fresh flowers in the bedrooms.

Invest in Some Basic Amenities for the Added Comfort of Your Guests

By increasing your nightly rate by just a few dollars, you can easily afford to offer a selection of complimentary but low-cost amenities that your guests will appreciate.

Some of these amenities can include:

▶ Several bottles of water, plastic cups, and coasters in the guestroom.
▶ A selection of travel-size toiletries (shampoo, conditioner, soap, toothpaste, mouth wash, skin cream, dental floss, cotton swabs, etc.) that you purchase from the dollar store, a pharmacy, or supermarket. Some travelers bring their own toiletries and won't use what you provide, but others

warning

Charging a higher nightly rate means inviting higher expectations from your guests. You can't get away with offering cheap, uncomfortable bed linens. Failure to offer accommodations that meet the guest's expectations will result in bad ratings and reviews, which will have a long-term detrimental impact on your success as an Airbnb host.

will appreciate having these items on hand. Each
guest should be provided with a new, unopened
selection of these amenities.

aha!

Think about the last
time you stayed at a
hotel or motel and what
complimentary amenities
were offered within the
guestroom. Try to offer as
many of these as possible.

- ▶ An ample supply of toilet paper in the bathroom,
  with a new roll in the toilet paper holder and at
  least two or three extra rolls where they're easily
  accessible to your guests, such as on a shelf or
  under the sink.
- ▶ A box of tissues in the bedroom (on the nightstand) and in the bathroom.
- ▶ A hair dryer.
- ▶ Iron and ironing board.
- ▶ Within the bathroom, make a can of Lysol or air freshener available.

If you're offering higher-end accommodations at a premium nightly rate, consider
including these additional amenities:

- ▶ Complimentary daily newspaper
- ▶ Fresh muffins and juice in the morning
- ▶ Access to a coffee machine with a premium selection of coffees and teas
- ▶ Down comforter on the bed, with a nice comforter cover that's easy to launder
- ▶ Television (with cable programming) in the bedroom
- ▶ Bottle of wine upon a guest's arrival
- ▶ Vase with fresh cut flowers in the guestroom
- ▶ Real wood furniture and/or antique furnishings that add elegance and character to
  the guestroom
- ▶ Guestrooms decorated and furnished around a theme, like Victorian, Contemporary,
  Tuscan style, Traditional, Coastal/Beach, Western/Rustic, Tropical, or Nautical
- ▶ Offer in-home gym/workout equipment, an in-home sauna, a hot tub, and/or other
  luxury equipment that your guests are able to use
- ▶ Include a fan, air conditioner, and/or portable heater in each guestroom, if neces-
  sary, so guests can control the temperature

As you choose furniture, décor, appliances, and consumer electronics to install
within the property and plan how you'll arrange the property and guestrooms,
consider ongoing maintenance issues—what will be involved with keeping everything
functional. Figure out who will handle the maintenance, and the cost of that ongoing
maintenance.

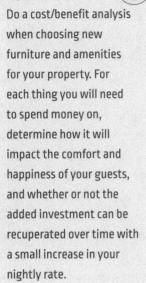

tip

Do a cost/benefit analysis when choosing new furniture and amenities for your property. For each thing you will need to spend money on, determine how it will impact the comfort and happiness of your guests, and whether or not the added investment can be recuperated over time with a small increase in your nightly rate.

Especially if you're catering to guests paying a premium nightly rate, everything within the property will be expected to be fully operational, so when something breaks, you'll need a plan in place to have it repaired quickly and affordably.

Buy Enough for Everyone

When stocking up on items that will be used consistently by your guests, make sure you acquire enough of everything for each guest, and have sufficient quantities of everything on hand if you wind up having guests back to back, and won't have time to go shopping or do laundry before your next guest arrives.

For example, for each bed, you'll need multiple sets of sheets, pillow cases, blankets, comforter covers, and pillows. For guests that stay a week, you might opt to launder the bedding one or two times during that period. However, if you'll be having one-night guests check in everyday, you'll need to strip the bedding between each guest and obviously provide clean and fresh bedding for each guest.

By utilizing a comforter cover, you can easy wash the cover between each guest and launder the actual comforter only once every few weeks, for example, especially if you're offering a flat top sheet as well.

For bedding, figure out how many sets of sheets, pillows, and blankets you'll need on hand for each bed, based on how frequently guests will be staying at your property and how often you plan to do laundry.

As for pillows, keep in mind that some people prefer more than one, and some people prefer down filling, while others require synthetic or cotton filling due to allergies, so for each bed, you'll want to have at least two or three pillows on hand, made from a selection of different materials.

tip

For sanitary reasons, seriously consider enclosing each of your mattresses in a plastic mattress cover that will keep bedbugs and bodily fluids, for example, from reaching the mattress itself. Also, refrain from utilizing decorative throw pillows on the bed or offering extra blankets that are made from materials that can't easily be laundered.

tip

Be sure to offer a laundry basket for guests to leave their used (dirty and wet) towels once they're done using them. If they'll be expected to reuse towels, be sure ample tower rack space is provided in the bathroom or guestroom, so the towels can dry off between uses and not get moldy.

Consider offering one bath towel, one hand towel, and one washcloth per guest, per day. Again, based on the number of guests you plan to have staying with you simultaneously, and how often you plan to do laundry, always have enough clean towels on hand, keeping in mind that periodically, a guest will have the need for extra towels.

Have enough dishes, coffee mugs, glasses, and silverware on hand in your kitchen so two or three meals can be served without having to do dishes. Then, stock up on disposable items, like garbage bags, selections of travel-size toiletries, toilet paper, tissues, dish soap, laundry detergent, and other necessities that you will continuously need on hand. Consider shopping at a wholesale club, like Costco or BJ's Wholesale Club, to save money, assuming you have the storage space available for the items you buy in bulk.

Offer a Detailed House Manual

In the previous chapter, we introduced the concept of creating a house manual (in addition to a list of house rules). While house rules provide guidelines for how guests are expected to act while staying at your property, a house manual is a document that outlines all of the most important information that your guests will need to know while they're staying with you. This printed document should be provided to your guests upon their arrival or can be placed within the guestroom where each guest will be staying.

Upon a new guest's arrival, you'll want to verbally go over the house rules, provide a tour, and offer brief demonstrations on how various things work. However, you can assume that only a small fraction of what you say will actually be remembered. This is why a house manual is important.

The house manual should include a printed copy of the house rules, as well as separate instructions for

aha!

Create a master shopping list for yourself with items you'll require on an ongoing basis and the quantity you need of each item. Then, in between shopping trips, update the list as needed. You can create the list on paper, or use a mobile app (such as Reminders on your smartphone or tablet).

operating equipment that could be confusing. This can include easy-to-understand, step-by-step directions for:

▶ Unlocking and locking the front door

▶ Turning on and using the television/home theater system, and operating the cable box (Also include a list of TV channels/networks you receive, and their corresponding channel numbers.)

▶ Using the washer and dryer

▶ Using the coffee machine

▶ Connecting to the in-home wifi

▶ Where it's OK to park and parking rules or local laws that guests need to adhere to

Also include answers to the most commonly asked questions you receive from guests, including:

▶ Have Restaurant Recommendations on Hand for Your Guests

Chances are, many of your guests will want to know your personal recommendations for nearby restaurants or bars or may want referrals about which restaurants deliver. Consider providing a detailed restaurant list, walking or driving directions to the most popular restaurants, as well as having a selection of menus on hand. This information should be included within your house manual.

In addition to the restaurants that offer their own delivery service, determine if your geographic area is serviced by mobile apps like Grubhub (www.grubhub.com), UberEats (www.ubereats.com), or Yelp Eat24 (http://eat24hours.com). These smartphone apps determine the user's location, locate all of the participating restaurants in the nearby area, displays menus for those participating restaurants, and then accepts orders to be delivered, whether or not the restaurant itself offers a delivery service.

Grubhub, UberEats, Yelp Eat24, and food delivery apps like them can be acquired for free from the App Store (iPhone/iPad) or the Google Play Store (Android smartphones and tablets). Once you determine one or more of these apps work in your geographic area, consider recommending them to your guests who are looking to have food or meals delivered.

If your property is within a region serviced by Amazon Prime Now, this too is a website (https://primenow.amazon.com) and mobile app that's worth recommending to your guests who need meals and/or nonfood items delivered.

- ▶ Directions to the closest grocery store, pharmacy, convenience store, and gas station
- ▶ A sampling of menus and walking/driving directions to a selection of popular restaurants that are nearby
- ▶ Information about popular attractions, landmarks, points of interest, and things to do in the area, including movie theaters

So that you can easily keep your house manual up to date, consider using a three-ring binder, and covering each topic on a separate page within the binder so you can easily update and replace specific sections or pages, without having to reprint the entire manual.

Be sure to include a copy of your house manual within each guestroom, and point it out during your initial tour. To serve its purpose, your house manual should be clearly written, comprehensive, well-organized, and easy to understand. It should also display your cell phone number prominently, so guests can call or text you with questions if you're not available in person.

tip

In addition to offering a detailed house manual, make it clear to your guests that you, as their host, are available to answer their questions or address their concerns in person. Make sure you provide guests with your cell phone number, so they can text you with questions during their stay or call you if their need is urgent. Once you start receiving the same question(s) repeatedly from guests, consider updating your house manual to include the appropriate answer(s).

Manage Your Time and Responsibilities

As a host, you'll have to do a series of tasks and chores daily, as well as complete a separate selection of important tasks after each guest leaves and before your next guest(s) arrives. You may also assign separate responsibilities to your professional cleaning service.

To ensure that you don't forget an important task or chore, write out detailed lists and schedules that include everything that needs to be done, and when. Include everything from laundry, washing dishes, sweeping the floors, and vacuuming the carpets to cleaning and sanitizing the bathroom, paying monthly bills (cable TV, utilities, landscaping, cleaning crew, etc.), replacing the bedding and making the beds between guests, and doing the necessary shopping.

Especially as a new host, it's essential that everything within your property always be clean, on hand, and ready for your guests. Remembering to do everything will require planning and organization on your part.

Cleaning and Preparing for Your Guests

To some extent, your guests should be expected to clean up after themselves from day to day and leave your property exactly how it was found when they first arrived. You'll discover, however, that your guests are not always so considerate or responsible.

Especially if you're renting one or more guestrooms in the home where you also live, as the host, you'll need to get into the habit of doing some basic cleaning on a daily basis whenever you have guests staying with you. Basic chores, like wiping down the bathroom, sweeping the floors, emptying trash cans, dusting, and making sure the dishes are clean, all become your responsibility.

If you're renting out an entire home or apartment for multiple nights, many of these basic housekeeping tasks can be left to your guests, provided you give them whatever is needed to handle them. Then, when each guest checks out, you will need to go into the property to clean up, sweep, vacuum, dust, change the bedding, clean and organize the bathroom, and prepare everything for the next guest.

warning

A guest should never have to look for a new roll of toilet paper in the bathroom, or come to you to report that you've run out of toilet paper. This, and situations like it, will virtually guarantee you receive a bad rating and review and cause serious inconvenience for your guests. It's your job as the host to do a daily inventory of all items on hand that could run out, and ensure there's always an ample supply of everything on hand, including: clean bath towels and toilet paper, coffee, bottled water, tea, and paper towels, for example.

aha!

If you're offering services or amenities that truly add value to someone's stay, consider building the cost of these extras into your published nightly rate, instead of listing extra fees for them within your property listing.

Depending on how much you're charging and how busy your schedule is, it may make financial sense to hire a professional maid service to come in one or more times per week, or in between guests, to give the property a proper and thorough cleaning. Choosing this option obviously costs money, but it also means you'll need to find and develop a business relationship with a trustworthy and reliable maid service.

In addition to an optional cleaning fee, Airbnb allows you to charge other extra fees but does not handle the collection of payment for them. For example, you could

▶ Should You Charge a Cleaning Fee?

Airbnb allows hosts to add an optional cleaning fee to their nightly rate. If you opt to charge this, your guests expect you to hire a professional cleaning company to ensure the property is clean, sanitized, and ready for them upon their arrival. Make sure you allow enough time in between bookings to properly clean your property. When each guest arrives, the property should be ready for them.

For your long-term guests (staying one week or longer), devise a cleaning schedule so they know what day(s) the bedding and towels, for example, will be laundered, and/or when the maid service will be visiting and need access to their guestroom or the property where they're staying.

If you're charging a premium rate for a guest to rent your entire property, adding a cleaning fee will likely be expected. However, if you're renting a single guestroom in a competitive marketplace, guests will likely baulk at an added cleaning fee, especially if you're one of the only hosts in the geographic area charging one.

To add an optional cleaning fee to your property listing, follow these steps:

1. From your computer, launch your web browser, and visit www.airbnb.com.
2. Sign in to your account.
3. From the Host menu, select the Manage Listings option.
4. Choose which listing you want to edit.
5. Click on the Pricing settings.
6. Under the Additional Pricing Options heading, add a checkmark to the checkbox that's labeled Cleaning Fee.
7. When prompted, enter the one-time cleaning fee you'd like to charge in conjunction with each reservation. This fee will be added to the reservation total but is listed separately. A separate host service fee is charged to you (the host) each time a cleaning fee is processed by the Airbnb service. (According to Airbnb, if a guest responds to a special offer when booking a reservation via your listing, the cleaning fee is not automatically added.)

charge a late check-in fee, pet fee, or bike rental fee, but these fees need to be disclosed within your property listing.

For more information on how to request payment for these fees, visit: www.airbnb.com/help/article/52/how-should-I-choose-my-listing-price. In general, charging extra fees is frowned upon by potential guests, and could result in someone viewing your listing but choosing a different host that does not charge the extra fee(s).

Attract Business Travelers with an Airbnb Business Travel Ready Listing

In addition to vacation or leisure travelers, Airbnb caters to business travelers by offering accommodations that meet a specific set of requirements that are designed to appeal specifically to business people traveling for work. Property listings that have earned a Business Travel Ready badge (which looks like a briefcase) are specifically set up to accept business traveler guests.

As an Airbnb host, you can apply to become a Business Travel Ready property, if you're offering an appropriate type of accommodation, the required selection of amenities, and you meet the other requirements outlined by Airbnb.

To see the most up-to-date list of requirements for becoming an Airbnb for Business host, visit: www.airbnb.com/business-travel-ready, and www.airbnb.com/help/article/1185/what-makes-a-listing-business-travel-ready.

Assuming your property qualifies, some of the additional services and amenities you'll need to provide as a host include:

▶ 24-hour check in
▶ Maintaining a strict no-smoking/no pets policy
▶ Offering business-friendly amenities, including: wifi, a laptop-friendly workspace, iron, hangers, hairdryer, and shampoo

The benefits as a host of earning the Airbnb Business Travel Ready badge are that your property listing will be showcased to business travelers, you'll wind up with more bookings, and you can typically charge a higher nightly rate. You'll also potentially receive more midweek or longer-term bookings, especially during nonpeak vacation periods.

Decide Whether or Not to Deal with Keys

Every time new guests arrives at your property, you'll need to provide them with an easy way to come and go as they please, 24 hours per day, during the length of their stay. One option is to provide them with a copy of the key(s) needed for entry, which you'll then need to collect upon each guest's checkout.

One problem with using a traditional key distribution method is that it becomes the guests' responsibility to lock the door after them each time they leave and not lose or forget the key, which will be needed to let themselves back in.

Available from any hardware store, you can replace the traditional key-entry locks on your front door with a digital smart lock that requires a numeric code for entry and that automatically locks itself each time the door is shut. No actual keys are required.

Some of the more advanced keyless-entry smart locks can be programmed and remotely controlled using a smartphone app, so as the host, you can quickly change the entry code as often as you like (in between guests, for example), from anywhere your smartphone has internet access.

These locks are available from a handful of manufactures. Most smart locks can be installed within 30 to 60 minutes on your own, using basic tools. However, any local locksmith can also install them. Once installed, some of these smart locks allow the host to use their smartphone or computer to track when guests come and go and ensure the door otherwise remains locked at all times. If someone forgets their code, the host can also remotely unlock the door using their internet-connected smartphone from virtually anywhere.

In addition to the keyless-entry smart locks that are available from your local hardware store, Airbnb has teamed up with a company called RemoteLock to offer a selection of keyless-entry smart door lock options specifically to Airbnb hosts. To learn more, visit http://remotelock.com/airbnb. Near the bottom of this web page, be sure to fill out the form to request the free white paper report, "Selecting the Right Smart Lock for Short-Term Rentals." As you'll discover, the cost of RemoteLock's offerings range from $249 to $469 per lock. (Keep in mind, less expensive options may be available from hardware stores and other online-based vendors.)

By utilizing these locks, you and your guests don't have to deal with traditional keys. You simply need to provide each guest with a numeric code to enter using the keypad in order to gain entry to your property. For the

save

To shop online for the selection of smart locks available from Home Depot, visit www. homedepot.com/s/ smartlocks. To shop for these locks online from Lowe's, visit: www.lowes. com/search?searchTerm= smart+locks. You'll also discover Amazon.com offers a vast selection of smart locks that can replace your existing door locks. To find them, visit www.amazon.com, and within the search field, enter the phase "smart locks."

► Meet Airbnb Hosts Gregory and Kristina Frankel

Some Airbnb hosts create a luxurious oasis for their guests, plus provide a living space that's truly unique and that incorporates the host's passions, skills, personal taste, and lifestyle. Husband and wife Gregory and Kristina Frankel are this type of Airbnb host. Their property is located in Michigan City, Indiana (near a state park and Lake Michigan), which is less than a 90-minute drive from downtown Chicago. Kristina describes the home as being very private.

"There is a gorgeous prairie in front of the house, woods in the back of the house, as well as a large garden on the property that can be seen from the house. I am a dance artist and choreographer, so we created a yoga/dance space within the home. The house is decorated in a modern way that melds the indoors and outdoors almost seamlessly. It has huge windows and is very open," explains Kristina. "We have kept the décor very simple, but highly functional and comfortable. You can stand or sit anywhere in this house and see something beautiful. It's all very peaceful."

Kristina and Gregory enjoy travel, but when they do, they typically seek out nontraditional accommodations in order to avoid staying at a generic hotel or motel. "When we got married and purchased our home, it was with the idea that we'd rent it out to paying guests. We wound up finding a really unique property that we fell in love with," explains Gregory. "Together, we had so much fun creating and decorating the space. We put a lot of effort into it, which is immediately apparent to our guests."

Kristina adds, "Our property is not just a home, it is a true sanctuary. I am a gardener, and Gregory enjoys cooking. When people stay with us and we're there, we serve farm-to-table meals. Using our own experiences traveling and being a guest at other Airbnb properties, we incorporated everything we learned when preparing our own property. Our own travels provided us with valuable insight into what works and what doesn't when preparing a home for paying guests."

One of the things that Gregory and Kristina pride themselves on is offering a truly beautiful living space, inside and out, while also offering unique on-site activities, as well as truly fresh dining experiences for their guests. "Part of the guest's experience is the hospitality my wife and I offer," adds Gregory. "We are natural hosts, and we treat our guests the same way we treat our best friends."

As part of the property's unique décor and amenities, one of the things that Gregory and Kristina boast that gets the best feedback from their guests is their record player and collection

► **Frankels,** continued

of vinyl records that guests can freely enjoy. Being amateur photographers and art collectors, the couple has decorated their property with their own photographs from exotic places that they've traveled to, along with artwork that they've collected from around the world.

By profession, Gregory is the creative director at an advertising agency that serves clients in the hospitality industry. He frequently used his creative skills and experience when decorating their home.

"We showcase the uniqueness of the property within the photos that appear as part of the Airbnb property listing. We took great care when composing the listing, so the types of guests who opt to stay with us tend to be like-minded people who want to experience sanctuary-like accommodations when they travel. Our guests have included young couples with kids from major cities, who want to give their kids a true country experience. We have also had many couples stay with us, as well as small groups of friends who travel together. Our style is so specific, it naturally draws like-minded people. Occasionally, we will welcome solo travelers . . . looking to relax, or who want a special space to create in," says Kristina.

Gregory adds, "When writing the property listing for Airbnb, I adopted a very engaging writing style that talks specifically to the type of guests that I'd want staying with us. Even after potential guests have seen the property photos and read the property listing, when they drive up to the house, the first words out of their mouths are typically, 'Oh my God, this place is amazing!' That's the response we wanted guests to have, right from the beginning, when we first decided to become Airbnb hosts."

Typically, when Gregory and Kristina are staying on the property with their guests, they always start off by giving new arrivals a complete tour. However, when the couple decides to travel, or if a guest wants to rent their entire place, they often rent out their entire home through Airbnb. The couple also maintains a nearby apartment where they themselves stay when the need arises.

"Our dream is to provide a creative space for people to come and create music, dance, art, or whatever their passion is. We provide the unique space, as well as the fresh farm-to-table meals," explains Kristina, who mentioned that when they first were real estate shopping, they paid careful attention to local laws in order to make sure the property they bought could be used for Airbnb hosting.

► **Frankels,** continued

Also prior to becoming an Airbnb host, the couple met with their accountant to ensure they'd be collecting and ultimately paying the appropriate taxes, based on the additional revenue they'd be earning. "For us, the most rewarding aspect of being Airbnb hosts is the opportunity to continuously meet new people and share our living space with them. Of course, we also like the revenue we earn," says Gregory.

Currently, Kristina and Gregory have set a nightly rate with Airbnb that includes the farm-to-table meals they serve when they are staying on the property with their guests. Separate pricing is also offered to guests who want to rent the entire property for themselves. "We are currently experimenting with different pricing options, based on what guests are looking for. Some guests don't want all of their meals prepared by us, so we're looking into offering a complete package price, as well as separate pricing for the accommodations and individual meals. We're still figuring out what works best," says Gregory.

In terms of offering tips to other Airbnb hosts about how to create the best possible listing, Gregory explains, "Showcasing great pictures within the property listing is essential. Then, try to tell a compelling story about the property and what you're offering as a host. Share what you personally love about the property. Figure out what the magic is about your place, and then find creative and truthful ways to share the experience people will have who will be staying in your home or at your property."

One mistake that Gregory made early on as an Airbnb host was relying on a cleaning lady to leave a house key in a certain location when she left, so the guests could let themselves in while Gregory and Kristina were traveling during the Thanksgiving holiday. The housekeeper forgot to leave a key, and there was no contingency plan in place for providing the guest with an alternate key.

"The guest arrived at the house, and there was no key to let themselves in. We had to track down someone who had a key, who was home that particular night, and who was able to get over to the house to let the guests in. Since then, we have developed multiple contingency plans for letting people into the house when they arrive if we're not there to greet them," says Gregory.

As Airbnb hosts, Gregory and Kristina accept guest bookings only from people who have verified personal profiles and previous positive reviews as Airbnb guests. "I turn down bookings

▶ **Frankels,** continued

periodically if I don't feel the guest will fit well within the living space we're offering," says Gregory. "I rely heavily on guests' past reviews when making my decision about whether or not to approve their booking request. Because our nightly rate is not cheap, that automatically weeds out most of the people who would not treat our home properly."

Prior to check out, Gregory and Kristina remind their guests to leave a review on Airbnb, but have found that most of the time, because of the experience they're offering, their guests are more than excited to leave a positive review, even without the reminder.

Gregory adds, "When we first started as Airbnb hosts, we strove to provide a lot of value, and then sought out feedback from our initial guests in order to ultimately set our nightly pricing. Every time we receive a booking request, I make a point to respond within an hour. I can do this from my smartphone, and our fast response time is one of the things we have specifically received very positive feedback about from our guests.

"We have added a cleaning fee for our guests, and have a professional cleaning lady come in to clean the house in between guests. However, on a day-to-day basis when we're here, we keep the house very clean ourselves. Out of all of the short-term rental services, we really like Airbnb because of the online community the service has built up, and their mobile app works really well. We have also listed our property with HomeAway, but have not found that service to be as user friendly for their hosts.

"Creating house rules and publishing them as part of your Airbnb listing is important. We also provide a printed-out version of the house rules as part of the house manual that we present to guests upon their arrival. Our house manual also describes where everything is located and offers some local recommendations for things to see and do in the area."

host and guests alike, this is typically a safer and more convenient option than a traditional key lock, and is well worth the additional investment.

New Hosts Should Hold a Dress Rehearsal

As a new travel host who has just made your property ready to invite guests, one of the optional things you can do to ensure everything will go smoothly with your paying guests is to hold a dress rehearsal. Just before you publish your Airbnb property listing, invite one or more of your close friends to stay with you and pretend to be an Airbnb guest. Have them stay in your guestroom(s), use your property, and experience everything that a paying guest would experience. Then, get their honest feedback, and make whatever adjustments are necessary.

You can also take this a step further, and have your friends book a paid stay at your property through Airbnb. This allows them to provide you, as the host, with your first review once their visit is complete. You can always reimburse your friends for the money they paid, and consider the fee you paid to Airbnb for the booking as a cost of doing business.

Either approach will allow you to practice being an Airbnb host, without the risk of making mistakes that could result in a bad review from a paying guest.

5

Responding to Broken Rules

Airbnb is successful because it's built a loyal and global online community that's comprises travelers and hosts. Whenever someone sets up an Airbnb account and plans to be a guest at someone's property, he or she agrees to adhere to basic rules of conduct. Likewise, hosts agree to follow Airbnb's guidelines and requirements for providing their paid guests with a clean, safe, and comfortable space to stay.

Airbnb's business model relies heavily on each user's willingness to follow the rules and to be respective, honest, and law abiding. For example, guests are expected to leave a host's property exactly how they found it and not steal anything or cause damage. They're also expected to follow the rules outlined by Airbnb and their host during their stay.

Most of the time, everyone follows these Airbnb-imposed guidelines, and the overall experience for the host and guests is a positive one. One incentive for following the rules is that hosts and guests both get to publish ratings and reviews about one another on the Airbnb service, and these reviews are available for all to see.

As a host, receiving bad reviews and low ratings is tantamount to your past guests warning your future guests against staying with you. Because the Airbnb community relies so heavily on reviews, it forces hosts to provide the best experience possible for their paying guests. Hosts with bad reviews don't get bookings. It's that simple.

warning

Should Airbnb guests wind up with many bad ratings and reviews, and/or have their account suspended by Airbnb, it's all too easy for that same person to simply create a new account, using an alternate email address, or someone else's information, for example. Thus, while ratings and reviews are a good indicator for what you, as a host, can expect from your guests, unfortunately this is not a foolproof system.

tip

Every day, millions of travelers stay with hosts based on bookings made through Airbnb and similar services, and the vast majority of bookings happen without a hitch. Chances are, this will be your experience as well. However, as a host, have plans in place to handle situations that go wrong.

Likewise, as a guest, receiving bad reviews and low ratings will prevent you from being able to use Airbnb in the future to book accommodations. Initially, you will be prevented from staying with hosts who have turned off the Instant Book feature, and who evaluate the ratings and reviews of their potential guests before accepting a booking. Then, after an account holder receives multiple negative reviews and ratings, Airbnb will often terminate that account altogether.

To help hosts and guests establish trust between parties, Airbnb has multiple features in place, including the review and rating system, the Verified ID system, and the Host Guarantee. As a member of the Airbnb community, once travelers establishe their free account, they have the ability to report (flag) any profile, property listing, or message

► If You Live Alone, Take Extra Precautions

If you're a host who is single, lives alone, and who will be renting out one or more guestrooms within a property where you're also living, it's important to always take extra precautions before inviting strangers into your home, regardless of what short-term rental service you're using. Sure, insurance will cover your property and belongings against theft or damage, but you also need to consider your own security and well-being.

This is where common sense and trust comes into play. As was discussed in previous chapters, as a host, you always have the ability to turn off the Instant Book feature. This requires potential guests to contact you and request a booking and gives you the opportunity to review their profile, read their past ratings and reviews, and have text-based correspondence with that potential guest before they show up to stay in your home.

As you review a potential guest's profile, ratings, and reviews, if for whatever reason you're not comfortable having that person stay with you, reject the booking request. Accept booking requests only from people you feel comfortable inviting into your home. Yes, this will result in potential lost revenue, but it will also help ensure your safety and peace of mind as a host.

In situations where you will be alone in your home with a stranger staying with you, have plans in place to protect your safety. For example, have a friend or neighbor check in on you, have a sturdy lock installed on your own bedroom door, and determine in advance exactly how you'll handle situations that make you uncomfortable or feel unsafe.

that they believe is offensive, discriminatory, that does not adhere to Airbnb's policies, or that they believe is suspicious.

Airbnb has a team in place that is responsible for investigating all content that is flagged by its users. While communicating with potential guests or booked guests via Airbnb's secure messaging service, either party always has the option to flag a message they receive that makes them uncomfortable or that they believe is inappropriate. Simply click on the flag icon to do this. However, if at any time

tip

Keep in mind, similar security and verification tools and features are offered by all other travel hosting services to help ensure the safety and security of travel hosts and guests alike. The more ways you (as a host) get verified, the more credibility you'll have, and the safer a potential guest will feel booking a reservation to stay with you.

you feel your safety or well-being is in jeopardy, or you're being threatened or harassed, call the police immediately.

Develop Clear House Rules That Leave No Room for Interpretation

The importance of developing a clear set of house rules has been discussed several times already. These rules need to be presented as part of your property listing on Airbnb and agreed to by your guests at the time they confirm their booking. You'll also want to verbally review the house rules upon your guests' initial arrival and have a printed copy of the house rules waiting for them in their guestroom (within the house manual, for example).

Assuming your guests are willing to adhere to their promise and obligation to follow your house rules, this should eliminate a lot of potential misunderstanding and problems. Remember, your house rules should be written in a way that protects you (the host), your property and belongings, as well as the other guests who are simultaneously staying with you (if applicable), and your neighbors.

It's important to understand that as a host, you are not allowed to utilize house rules as a way to discriminate against potential guests or paying guests. Airbnb has a firm policy against publishing any content within your profile or property listing, for example, that promotes hatred, racism, discrimination of any kind, harassment, or harm against any individual or group.

In addition to this blanket policy, hosts must adhere to all of their local, state, and federal laws pertaining to discrimination, which in the United States, for example, includes what's mandated within the Fair Housing Act and Americans with Disabilities Act. For more information, visit: www.airbnb.com/help/article/483/airbnb-s-nondiscrimination-policy.

Consider Requesting a Security Deposit

One of the options you have as an Airbnb host to help protect your property and belongings, is to request a security deposit from your guests when they book and pay for their reservation.

aha!

As you're creating your list of house rules, check a handful of other property listings from Airbnb hosts who have received a lot of positive ratings and reviews and have earned the Superhost accreditation. These hosts have updated and tweaked their house rules over time, based on their own firsthand experiences dealing with guests, and may give you good ideas about rules you'll want to adopt that relate to your unique concerns and property.

This is a predetermined amount of money, between $95.00 and $5,100 (USD). If necessary, Airbnb will collect the fee on your behalf. However, you need to prove that a guest damaged your property or belongings to collect any money from a guest's security deposit.

To add or edit a security deposit requirement for your property listing, visit the Airbnb website using your computer's web browser, sign into your account, click on the Manage Listings option under the Host menu, select the property listing you wish to edit, and then click on the Pricing Settings option. From below the Additional Pricing Options heading, add a checkmark to the checkbox associated with the Security Deposit option, and then enter the amount you wish to charge.

The newly added security deposit requirement will apply only to reservations booked after you have added this option to your listing. This type of payment must be handled through Airbnb's website, or it is considered a violation of terms on the part of the host.

If it becomes necessary for a host to claim part or all of a guest's security deposit, the claim must be made within 14 days of the guest's checkout date, or according to Airbnb's website, "Before a new guest checks in, whichever is easier." Once a claim is made, Airbnb will mediate and collect the payment from the guest, as required.

As a host, once you initiate a claim, be prepared to provide Airbnb with written documentation that offers proof of your financial loss or damage to your property. Documentation and proof may include photos or video, along with receipts, invoices, and/or written estimates. Ultimately, Airbnb will determine how much of the security deposit you should be paid, based on your financial loss or damage.

Keep in mind, when you require a security deposit from your guests, this becomes part of your property listing. Some potential guests may frown upon this and seek out another property to stay at that does not have this requirement. However, especially if you're offering a higher-end property that's filled with expensive furniture and décor, you may decide that requiring a security deposit is in your best interest as a host, even if it ultimately leads to slightly fewer bookings.

To learn more about how the security deposit system works, visit: www.airbnb.com/help/article/352/what-happens-if-a-host-makes-a-claim-on-my-security-deposit.

What to Do When Guests Don't Follow Your Rules or Something Inappropriate Happens

Your experiences as an Airbnb host will hopefully be consistently good ones. However, if you wind up welcoming a guest who doesn't follow your rules, who places you in a dangerous situation, or who causes damage to your property, you'll want to take immediate action. The safety of yourself, your family, your pets, your neighbors, and your property must always come first and be your primary concern.

Depending on the severity of the situation, what house rules have been broken, and the behavior of your guest, you typically have several options when dealing with a problem, including:

tip

If at any time you feel like you're in danger, call your local police or dial 911 immediately, and if possible, leave the property, and wait in a safe location for the authorities to arrive.

- ▶ Ignore the minor infraction, and simply deal with it. Then wait for the guest to check out on their prearranged date. If necessary, you can file a claim with Airbnb or your insurance company to recover a financial loss due to damage caused by your guest.
- ▶ Have a discussion with your guest. Provide a friendly reminder that they have violated a house rule, and give them a chance to apologize and remedy the situation.
- ▶ Report the violation to Airbnb, and follow the directions you're provided. How to do this is explained shortly. If necessary, impose an additional fee to compensate you for any expenses incurred cleaning or repairing your belongings or property.
- ▶ Evict the guest from your property prior to their planned checkout date. Do this by following the guidelines provided by Airbnb.
- ▶ Call the police or dial 911 immediately. Obviously this is the most drastic measure.

▶ Consider Acquiring Optional Short-Term Rental Insurance

For protecting your property and belongings, and having appropriate liability insurance in place for your property, along with traditional homeowner's or renter's insurance, a handful of insurance companies have begun offering specialized short-term rental insurance that's designed specifically for travel hosts who have paying guests staying in their home. One of the first companies to offer short-term rental insurance is Comet Insurance. To learn more about its insurance offerings, visit: www.comethome.com, or call (650) 799-0213.

To learn more about the host protection insurance and host guarantee that's automatically provided to hosts by Airbnb, visit: www.airbnb.com/host-protection-insurance and www.airbnb.com/guarantee. Understand that while the descriptions for these host protections sounds good, they may not fully cover you from a financial loss if a problem actually occurs. Having your own insurance as well is definitely a smart strategy.

Which option you choose should obviously be based on the severity of the situation, whether you (or your family, pets, other guests, or neighbors) have been put in harm's way, and/or whether the guest's actions have resulted in financial loss for you and/or damage to your property.

If possible, try to approach the situation with a business mindset, as opposed to an overly emotional one, and understand you always have the ability to write a strong negative review about that guest once he or she leaves, plus provide him or her with a low rating.

How to Report Violations of Your House Rules to Airbnb

Prior to or during guests' stay at your property, you have the option to decline or cancel their reservation, if a guest violates one or more of your house rules. However, you must follow the guidelines provided by Airbnb to do this.

Airbnb has published a series of detailed standards and expectations policies on its website (www.airbnb.com/standards) to which everyone—guests and hosts alike—is expected to adhere. As a host, familiarize yourself with these policies that relate to safety, security, fairness, authenticity, and reliability.

To report a violation by a guest, or provide documentation when canceling a guest's reservation due to an extenuating circumstance, go to Airbnb's website, and utilize the Contact Us option (www.airbnb.com/help/contact_us). From below the Resolve an Issue heading, you will see the prompt, "What is your question about?" Click on the Hosting option. At the "What can we help you with?" prompt, select Alterations and Cancelations, Safety, or whichever option from the pull-down menu is most appropriate to your issue. Follow the onscreen prompts and the directions or recommendations that the Airbnb service provides.

warning

If Airbnb's system notices that are you declining many booking requests, this could negatively affect your property listing's search result placement on the Airbnb service. If you have accepted a reservation request and then canceled it, you could be subject to cancelation penalties and become ineligible for Superhost status, unless the reason for cancelation is considered by Airbnb to be an "extenuating circumstance." To avoid penalties, document your reason for canceling a guest's confirmed reservation. Acceptable reasons include: maintenance issues that will impact your ability to host; death of a family member; serious illness; severe property damage; natural disasters; or political unrest.

Alternatively, from your internet-connected computer, visit Airbnb's Resolution Center (www.airbnb.com/resolutions_center) in order to send or request money for refunds, services, or damages related to your reservations. For this feature to work, as a host, there must be an eligible reservation within the Airbnb system.

If you're trying to recover money from a guest who has caused damage, for example, from the Resolution Center, click on the Request Money button, and then follow the on screen prompts. You have 30 days after a guest's checkout date to pursue this option.

tip

You always have the option to call Airbnb's Customer Service phone number, which is available 24 hours per day, seven days per week. The phone number is (855) 424-7262 or (415) 800-5959. If you choose this option, you may be subjected to an on-hold wait before you can speak with a human.

How to Evict a Guest from Your Property

Assuming you're not in danger, but a guest refuses to leave, one option as a host is to contact Airbnb via its website (www.airbnb.com/help/contact_us) or by phone, and then follow their recommendations in order to get a guest to leave peacefully. If your need to evict a guest is more pressing, or you feel you're in danger, contact the police.

What If the Problem Is Your Fault?

If, as a host, you make a mistake that impacts the quality of your guest's stay, try to rectify the situation during your guest's stay in order to avoid a negative review.

However, if someone is injured on your property, it's essential that you make sure the guest receives the medical attention required, and that you document everything that happens. If the guest refuses medical attention after an injury, have him or her put this in writing.

Once an incident happens, immediately create a detailed timeline, write everything down, take pictures, and try to find people who witnessed the events that led to the incident and the incident itself. Work with the local authorities as necessary, and consult with your lawyer, insurance company, and Airbnb as soon as possible.

What to Do If You Become a Victim of Airbnb-Related Fraud

While Airbnb-related fraud is not a common occurrence, it has been known to happen all over the world. For example, fraud occurs if a guest tries to extort money or a free stay from the host for any reason that is based on lies. In some cases, guests have been known to use the threat of a bad review in order to extort money or a free stay from the host.

According to Airbnb's website, "By posting a review, you agree to follow all Airbnb guidelines and policies, including the Extortion Policy, which Airbnb may enforce at our sole discretion. Failure to do so may result in the restriction, suspension, or termination of your Airbnb account." To learn more about Airbnb's Extortion Policy, visit: www.airbnb.com/help/article/548/what-is-airbnb-s-extortion-policy.

aha!

Keeping all of your personal, financial, tax-related, and legal paperwork and files off property, at another residence, within an in-home safe, or within a local bank's safety deposit box is a smart strategy.

Another rare issue that's been reported by Airbnb hosts is that guests invade the designated private areas of the host's property when the host is not home. One reason why a guest might invade a host's privacy is to steal or make copies of personal documents that provide the information needed for identity theft or other types of financial fraud. As a host, consider investing in a personal safe, or keep financial documents, credit card statements, bank statements, your passport, and other legal documents locked up and away from where they can easily be viewed or taken by a guest. If someone is renting your entire property, put your incoming personal mail on hold or have your personal mail diverted to a post office box (as opposed to having it delivered to your actual address).

tip

Invest in a paper shredder, and use it to destroy any paper-based documentation that you ultimately want to throw away. Don't just leave documents, bills, or bank statements, for example, that you plan to discard in a trash can that your guests have access to.

If a guest gains access to your personal, legal, tax-related, and/or financial documents, this could lead to identity theft, credit card fraud, or other problems that you might not discover right away. In addition to storing these documents in a secure way, add password protection to your desktop and laptop computer(s), turn on the features that prevent guest users from installing or deleting software onto that computer, or, better yet, prevent guests from using any computers where you have personal, financial, or legal documents stored or from which you handle your personal finances or online banking, for example.

Another way to help protect yourself as a host is to initially communicate only with potential guests via Airbnb's secure messaging system. Until the potential

▶ Meet Real Estate and Short-Term Rental Expert Ross Milroy

Ross Milroy, a real estate expert and financial specialist based in Miami Beach, Florida, has become extremely familiar with the short-term rental business in recent years. He became interested in short-term rentals when he discovered that a growing number of cities and states across the United States are starting to regulate and in some cases prevent hosts from legally offering their property as a short-term rental through a service such as Airbnb.

In this section, Milroy shares his knowledge about short-term rentals and offers advice about how to become a successful host using a service like Airbnb. The advice and tips he offers are based on his own opinions and experiences, which may or may not apply to your specific situation. To learn more about Ross Milroy and his services, visit www.rossmiami.com.

"What initially brought short-term rental laws to my attention was when I read the Miami Beach ordinance that came up in 2010. Several of my investment clients, who owned real estate in Miami Beach that was used to generate revenue via short-term rentals, approached me to determine what recourse they had. This was the first time I had heard about a local municipality, in this case, Miami Beach, trying to regulate short-term rentals.

"My clients felt that the ordinance was an intrusion by the city on their property rights. In 2016, the ordinance was updated and significant changes were made. Fines for violating the ordinance were increased from $500.00 to $15,000 for a first offence. The maximum fine is now up to $100,000. Real estate investors who were interested in owning a home in Miami Beach, and then generating income from it through short-term rentals when they themselves were not using the property, have been directly impacted in a negative way by these regulations.

"Once some of my real estate investors learned about the local ordinances in place, they had to walk away from otherwise excellent real estate investment opportunities in Miami Beach. At the end of the day, the investors were not comfortable with the local regulation pertaining to short-term rentals," explains Milroy.

While publically, the municipalities claim that these ordinances are being put in place for the safety and well-being of the community, Milroy believes the true reason for the ordinances is to protect a select group of wealthy homeowners who are lobbying the city to prevent short-term rentals, and the coming and going of people staying at short-term rental properties, which could have a negative impact on real estate prices in the community.

"The irony is that if you do a search for Airbnb properties to stay at in Miami Beach, you'll find over 1,000 listings, even though short-term rentals are technically no longer permitted," says

► **Milroy,** continued

Milroy. "A huge number of people are still illegally renting. When you list your property as a host on Airbnb, for example, your name and property address is not disclosed until after a paid reservation is made. As a result, the government officials in charge of upholding the ordinance don't always go through the hassle of booking reservations in order to figure out who the violating hosts are, in their efforts to enforce the ordinance. This is how some people are opting to work around the local ordinances."

Even if no local or state government ordinances are in place to prevent someone from using their property for short-term rentals as a way to earn money, Milroy warns that condominium owners and people living within a housing community must also adhere to the rules published by their coop board or homeowner's association, and that many of these organizations prohibit short-term rentals or subleases of any kind.

"Make sure you understand the occupancy restrictions that are in place for the property you plan to offer as a short-term rental. The problems start at some properties when neighbors begin complaining about all of the transient guests that are moving in and out of the short-term rental property. Before getting involved with Airbnb as a host, do your research. One of the first things you can do is online research," says Milroy.

"If you're dealing with a condominium complex, for example, you must carefully review the condominium documents. In the state of Florida, condominium documents are all public record and can be accessed online," he adds.

Unless you're comfortable reading and understanding what are often complex legal documents, consider hiring a real estate attorney to review the necessary documents on your behalf in order to determine whether or not you're allowed to host paying guests through a service like Airbnb. First and foremost, however, before signing up as a host with Airbnb (or any other service), make sure you're legally able to do so. Then, take steps to ensure that your neighbors and others in your community will not be negatively impacted by the coming and going of your transient guests.

"Based on my own experience representing property owners who offer their properties for short-term rental through Airbnb versus HomeAway, I have seen that Airbnb attracts a younger demographic of guests, who are more apt to cause property damage or have noise complaints issued against them, compared to older and more established guests who use a service like HomeAway to rent a vacation property to stay at," says Milroy.

▶ **Milroy,** continued

"If you're going to rent through Airbnb, I would not furnish the property with very expensive furniture, artwork, or appliances. Instead, my advice is to focus on being more of a budget host, and focus on volume, as opposed to becoming a host looking to charge premium pricing for a longer-term rental that lasts a week or longer. Keeping in mind the type of guests you'll be hosting, make your property dummy proof," he adds.

Again, based on the experience Milroy has had representing clients who offer their properties for short-term rental, he recommends that hosts strive to provide consistently good service. He explains, "Regardless of how much your guests are paying, be there for [them]. One bad review can have a negative impact on your long-term success. As a host, you live and die based on your reviews. You can't buy good reviews and ratings. You must earn them. There is an art to earning good reviews and getting your guests to voluntarily publish an optional review about their experience once they've stayed with you. Learning how to extract positive reviews from your guests will play a huge role in your success as a host.

"One way to earn positive reviews is to make it clear when someone checks in that you want to make their stay as comfortable as possible. Then, after a day or two, check in with them to ensure their stay is going well. When you know you have achieved your goal, and your guest has had a positive stay, as they're checking out, remind them to post a review about their experience."

Milroy also strongly recommends paying attention to safety related to your property. "You need to dummy-proof it," he explains. "Don't provide an infant highchair, for example. If someone comes with a baby, and that guest damages the chair, or uses it improperly, resulting in a child getting injured, you can be held accountable. You need to be very careful about what you put in the property and what you make available to your guests. This includes anything that's flammable or that contains glass. Especially if you opt to invite families to stay with you, you must child-proof the property.

"How you furnish and decorate your property, and showcase it in photos as part of your property listing, will directly impact the type of guests that opt to stay with you. At the end of the day, people will judge you and your property by the location, price, the image you convey, and by your reviews. Each of these things are important and relevant and should be considered carefully. Then, if you plan to become a host and make it a business, find the best way to manage it.

▶ **Milroy,** continued

"I believe that the best way to start off as a host is to rent out one or more rooms within your home, as opposed to an entire property. One of the best Airbnb places I ever stayed, however, was in Colorado, where the property owner built a separate apartment over their home's garage. Based on the design of this apartment, and the fact that he is on hand to manage it and serve as a good host, he's able to consistently rent it via Airbnb more than 300 days per year and charge $180.00 per night.

"Once you become successful as a host renting out a single property, you can always branch out and acquire additional investment properties that you'll rent out through Airbnb or a similar service. However, once you start trying to manage multiple properties, you really need to hire a professional management company that will represent you as if they were representing their own properties," says Milroy.

guest actually books and pays for a reservation, Airbnb does not disclose your address, phone number, last name, or any other personal information about you.

If it becomes necessary to communicate with your paying guests on a more personal level, refrain from sharing too much information about yourself or providing details about your life that a potential criminal could use for identity theft or other fraudulent purposes. For example, be extremely cautious if a guest asks questions like, "Where do you do your banking?" or "How and where do you manage your retirement account or investment account?"

Communication Is Essential

As an Airbnb host, you have many opportunities to communicate with your prospective and booked guests, using text messaging, through phone conversations, and ultimately in person once the

warning

Whether or not a local or state government will strictly uphold ordinance that prevents hosts from using their property for short-term rentals can vary greatly and could change at any moment. Regardless of what advice you're given from the Airbnb website (or any other short-term rental service you opt to use), make sure you fully understand the current local laws and ordinances that are in place related to your geographic area before offering your property as a short-term rental.

guest arrives at your property. Each time you have an interaction with a (prospective) guest, you have the opportunity to create a positive experience, or you can conduct yourself in a way that's off-putting and unprofessional. The choice is yours, and the result of each communication will ultimately contribute to whether or not someone offers you a booking, and then whether or not you receive a positive review and rating from that guest.

Thus far, you've read a handful of strategies that can help you consistently offer your guests top-notch hospitality. In the next chapter, more emphasis is put on how you should communicate and interact with people as an Airbnb host.

6

Best Practices for Communicating with Guests

In addition to offering a clean, comfortable, and safe place to stay for your guests, good communication and hospitality skills are probably the most important talents you can possess if you want to be a host who consistently earns great reviews.

Becoming a host is something you have chosen to do, and it's a job that comes with a handful of responsibilities.

Communicating and interacting with your guests in a positive, helpful, and unobtrusive way is among those responsibilities.

By clearly and honestly conveying information in a friendly way, right from the start of each interaction you have with a prospective guest, you can easily avoid misunderstandings and help to ensure that each guest's stay goes as smoothly as possible. Doing this also benefits you, because as the host, you'll experience less hassle and have a much higher chance of earning positive reviews.

As a host, your communication and hospitality skills are used when creating your personal profile and property listing, because what you write sets a tone and allows your potential guests to set expectations for their upcoming stay.

Then, you'll have the opportunity to communicate with your (potential) guests many other times, including:

▶ During the inquiry process (via Airbnb's online messaging system), when a potential guest can ask questions.

▶ During the reservation booking process (also via Airbnb's online messaging system), when a potential guest requests a booking, assuming you have Airbnb's Instant Book feature turned off.

▶ Once a reservation has been made, when you need to coordinate with the guests when they'll arrive, plus answer any additional questions they have.

▶ When your guests arrive at your property and you welcome them in person, provide a tour, and help them get settled in. This is best done in person by you, or someone acting as your representative, but as you'll learn shortly, it can be done other ways, too.

▶ Throughout your guests' stay you can (and should) check in with them periodically to see how their stay is going, determine if they need anything, and ask if they have any questions or concerns. You can do this in person, by phone, or by text message, for example. Depending on each guest's preferences, and the expectations you've set, you can be as involved as you'd like during a guest's stay by offering

> **tip**
>
> Communication skills refers to all aspects of interaction you have with your prospective guests prior to their booking, upon their arrival, throughout their stay, and when they check out. This communication can happen using Airbnb's online messaging system, via email, through text messaging, on the telephone, by leaving handwritten notes for your guests during their stay, and of course, in person. If you're working with another travel hosting service, you will also be provided with a variety of similar ways to communicate with your (potential) guests.

your services as a tour guide, dining companion, or informal concierge who is on hand to answer questions beyond the scope of their stay at your property.

▶ During the checkout process. This too should ideally be done in person by you or someone representing you, but it can be done in other ways as well.

In most cases guests are paying much less to stay at your property than they'd have to pay to stay at a hotel, motel, or bed-and-breakfast, so, as the host, you're not expected to offer the same level of personalized attention, service, and hospitality. After all, people who work at these places have had professional training in order to serve in the hospitality industry.

However, your guests will often welcome communication with you and the hospitality you offer and will typically reward these extra efforts by providing you with an excellent rating and review (assuming the property itself meets or exceeds their expectations).

Airbnb's Secure Messaging System

Airbnb's secure online messaging system is provided for a number of important reasons. First, it allows (potential) guests and hosts to communicate using a real-time text messaging system, without having to reveal any personal information about themselves, such as their last name, phone number, or address. It's also convenient. One party can send a message, and the other party can respond instantly, or at their leisure, yet it's possible to have a full conversation and exchange important information.

For everyone's safety and security, the messaging system also maintains a complete record of every conversation that transpires, so you can easily look back and remember what you've discussed, or have proof to show to Airbnb or the authorities if someone says something offensive, threatening, or inappropriate.

While you're engaged in a text messaging conversation, as a host, it's possible to view a guest's full profile and past reviews, view their payment details and reservation dates, see your own availability calendar, and quickly see things like reservation confirmations, pre-approvals, special offers, or the rate a (prospective) guest is or will be paying. Also while engaged in a conversation via the messaging service, a host has the ability to handle administrative tasks, like accepting or declining a reservation request.

fun fact

A message thread is a conversation between two parties that's displayed in the order that the messages were sent and received. A complete conversation transcript is created and viewable. Each conversation you have with a specific person is stored as a separate message thread, so you can quickly switch between conversations.

This communication option becomes available the instant a potential guest sends an inquiry to a host or submits a reservation request. To use this service, it is necessary to be logged in to your Airbnb account via the website or mobile app. In fact, anyone can freely switch between logging in to Airbnb via their internet-connected computer's web browser and the mobile app, and all messaging content will remain up to date.

To access the messaging system, click on the Messages option, and then from your Inbox, click on the message thread for the text message conversation you want to participate in. From the Messages option, you can respond to any incoming message, compose and send a new message, or go back and review older messages (or complete message threads).

It's important to understand that this method of communication is not designed to manage lengthy conversations. In fact, each message thread allows only for 30 separate messages to be composed and sent by each party within a 24-hour period.

Often, when people use a messaging service, like Facebook Messenger, to communicate with their friends or family members, they use emoticons, cute abbreviations, or sentence fragments within their messages, and this is appropriate and acceptable. Keep in mind, when you're communicating with potential or actual guests, this is for business purposes, so your conversation should be friendly, but adopt a more professional approach that's void of emoticons and abbreviations like "LOL" (laugh out loud) or "TTYL" (talk to you later).

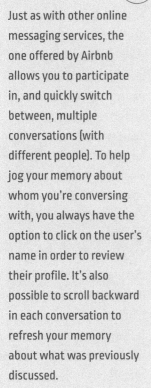

tip

Just as with other online messaging services, the one offered by Airbnb allows you to participate in, and quickly switch between, multiple conversations (with different people). To help jog your memory about whom you're conversing with, you always have the option to click on the user's name in order to review their profile. It's also possible to scroll backward in each conversation to refresh your memory about what was previously discussed.

Try to use full sentences and phrasing that allow you to convey as much information as possible, in a way that's easy to understand and not open for interpretation or misunderstanding. Also, as a host, focus on providing the fastest response time possible, so your (potential) guests do not have to wait for multiple hours (or longer) to receive an answer to an important question, for example.

One of the nice features offered by the Airbnb messaging system is that it allows you to receive a push notification (alert or text message) on your smartphone, each time a new incoming message or response to a previous message is received. To turn on this feature from within the Airbnb app, launch the app, and tap on the Profile icon. Select the Settings option, followed by Notifications option, and then follow the on-screen prompts to turn on or off the Notifications feature.

To use the Airbnb website to turn on push notifications, log in to Airbnb via your computer browser, click on your name that appears in the top-right corner of the browser window, and then click on the Account option, followed by the Notifications option. Next, click on the Mobile Notifications/Text Messages option, and follow the on-screen prompts to turn on or off these features.

Keep in mind that receiving text message alerts about new messages works only in North America and Europe, and standard messaging/data rates charged by your cellular service provider may apply. The push notifications feature will work with any internet-enabled smartphone or tablet. It can be adjusted via the Settings option on your mobile device.

For example, on an iPhone or iPad, launch Settings, tap on the Notifications option, and then tap on the app

tip

A push notification or text message will be sent to your smartphone when you turn on Airbnb's Notifications feature. This means you don't have to constantly log into and check the Airbnb website or mobile app for new messages. Instead, you'll be alerted as soon as one is received. Once you receive a notification or text message, respond to the message as quickly as possible.

listing for Airbnb from the Notifications menu. It's then possible to turn on or off notifications for the Airbnb app, plus determine if these notifications will be displayed within the Notification Center, whether they'll generate a sound, be displayed as a badge (as part of the Airbnb app icon on the device screen page), and/or be displayed on the lock screen. You can also set up a notification to be displayed as a banner or alert on your smartphone or tablet, so it appears on the screen regardless of what other function you are doing on the device.

Get to Know Your Guests Before They Check In

Before guests actually arrive at your property to check in, the Airbnb messaging service offers a secure and somewhat informal way to interact with these people. As the host, it's important you be honest when responding to questions or concerns. However, you can also use this communication as an opportunity to get to know your guests in advance, by asking them questions and holding short, friendly conversations.

Without delving too deeply into someone's privacy, you can pose questions like:

▶ Have you ever been to this area before?

▶ What is the main reason for your visit?

▶ Do you want some advice about the fun things do to while you're here, so you can make advanced reservations and plan your itinerary?

▶ What are some of the things you plan to do while you're here?

▶ Would you be interested in spending some time during your stay so I can be your informal tour guide and show you around the area?

▶ As your host, I am happy to serve breakfast each morning or have muffins and coffee on hand. Is this something you're interested in?

▶ Do you have any special needs or allergies that I should know about that relates your stay?

▶ What are your favorite hobbies?

warning

Airbnb does not permit hosts or guests to solicit the exchange of money directly between two parties. Any money that's exchanged (to pay for a reservation, cleaning fee, security deposit, or anything else) must go through Airbnb's service. If a guest tries to extort money from you for any reason via the messaging system, or if a message is received that is inappropriate or threatening, immediately flag that message by clicking on the flag icon, and then do not continue communicating with that person until you have consulted with Airbnb.

You can also use this pre-arrival communication to share information with your pending guests. For example, if they'll have a car, you can tell them where they should park when they arrive and what the local parking rules are. You can also ask questions about what time they'll be arriving, so you can be on hand to welcome them.

Welcome Guests in Person

Many hosts believe that it's important to be on hand at their property when guests first arrive. This allows the host to meet their guests in person and handle some important tasks, including:

aha!

Immediately upon their arrival, most guests will appreciate it if you offer them a bottle of water as you welcome them. If a guest is paying top-dollar to rent your entire property for a week or longer, you might also consider giving them a bottle of wine as a welcome gift.

- ▶ Providing a tour of the property
- ▶ Reviewing the house rules
- ▶ Helping guests settle in
- ▶ Providing front door keys (or a keyless-entry code) so guests can then come and go as they please
- ▶ Assist the guests in carrying their luggage to their guestroom

During the initial welcome, be sure to make your guests feel as comfortable as possible, and make it clear that you're available to answer their questions or address any concerns they have. At the conclusion of the property tour, ask if guests need anything right away, or if they anticipate needing extra blankets, pillows, or towels, for example. Also inquire if the guestroom temperature is comfortable for them, and let them know how to adjust the temperature, if possible.

Other Ways to Welcome Your Guests

If, for whatever reason, you can't be on hand to welcome your guests when they first arrive, you have two options. First, have a representative (who you trust) welcome them. Second, you can pre-arrange how and where guests will obtain a key to the property, and then provide them with a detailed welcome letter and house manual that provides all of the information they need to know. You can then follow up with a phone call to ensure they've arrived and settled in smoothly.

This second option is the least personal but is typically used if you're renting out a vacation home or secondary property that is nowhere near your primary residence. Should you opt to utilize this method, have multiple contingency plans in place in case there's a problem upon their arrival that requires in-person attention.

Interacting with Guests During Their Stay

Whether you're living at the property and sharing it with your guests, or your guests have rented your entire property for one day, several days, a week, or longer, maintaining an open line of communication with them is essential. It's important that you make your guests feel comfortable contacting you with their questions, problems, or concerns, before and during their stay.

For example, if your guests are staying in a guestroom that they find too hot or too cold at night, and this impacts their quality of sleep, they need to feel comfortable asking you how to adjust the temperature or for alternate types of bedding and blankets, in order to rectify the situation. As the host, if you're nowhere to be found, and guests are not comfortable calling or texting you, and they're forced to be uncomfortable during their stay, this will ultimately be held against you when they write their review. However, this is an example of a problem that could easily be addressed and fixed, if you're accessible.

Within the house manual, as well as verbally when your guest arrives, make it crystal clear that you're available by phone, in person, or text message (whichever apply), if they need anything whatsoever. If you work during the day, or are unreachable during specific hours, make this clear upfront. Then, make a point to check in periodically with your guests during a break at work, in order to respond to their messages as quickly as possible.

In addition to waiting for your guests to reach out to you, plan to initiate contact with them periodically during their stay. For example, when they wake up, be on hand in the kitchen or living room to say "good morning" and offer them some coffee. As they're going out for dinner in the evening, ask how their stay is going, and determine if they need anything.

If you suspect your guest does need something, and you can predict this need, offer it before they have the opportunity to ask. Understanding and anticipating the wants, needs, and concerns of your guest will help you become an excellent host.

tip

Having someone who represents you, such as a neighbor or property manager, welcome your guests is less personal than handling this task yourself. Make sure the person who will greet your guests is friendly, knowledgeable about the property, reliable, and equipped to handle any situations that may arise, including an unexpected early or late arrival by your guest.

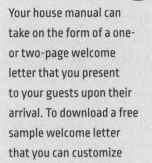

tip

Your house manual can take on the form of a one- or two-page welcome letter that you present to your guests upon their arrival. To download a free sample welcome letter that you can customize to include your own property's information, visit: www.airbnbguide. com/sample-airbnb-guest-welcome-sheet-download.

Keep in mind, there's a big difference between being available and attentive and being intrusive. If your guests want to be left alone and have minimal interaction with you, respect their wishes, but also be attentive to providing what they need. In this situation, perhaps leave a handwritten note on their bed (or attached to the outside of their guestroom door) that says, "I hope you're enjoying your stay thus far. Please let me know if you need anything." Be sure to include your cell phone number within the note.

If you sense that a guest wants to spend time chatting or join you for a meal, for example, consider extending a friendly invitation, as long as it will not be perceived as an unwanted sexual advance. Some hosts take on the same role as someone who runs a professional bed-and-breakfast and go out of their way to provide ongoing, professional-level hospitality, as well as personalized service and extra amenities during a guest's stay. Others focus on their core responsibilities as a host—to provide a clean, comfortable, and safe place to stay—but are less social with their guests during the length of their stay.

Again, how much interaction you have, and when this interaction takes place, is a matter of what you're willing to offer, while respecting your guests' wishes and needs. Look for subtle cues from your guests in terms of what their expectations are from you as the host, and then do your best to meet or exceed those expectations.

How to Offer Additional Customer Service and Amenities

Depending on how much your guests are paying per night, what information you included within your property profile, and what expectations your guests have developed, in addition to whatever amenities you've promised within the property listing, you always have the option of offering additional amenities on a complementary basis.

tip

Often saying something as simple as, "Good morning," "How is your afternoon going?" or "Are you comfortable in your guestroom; do you need any additional pillows or blankets?" will go a long way toward making a guest feel good about having you as a host.

► Meet Airbnb Host and B&B Operator Nadine Fox

Nadine Fox, who works as a teacher, and her husband, who is a cowboy, have been operating what they describe as a "guest ranch in Pennsylvania" for more than 32 years. "It's more than a traditional bed-and-breakfast, because we also offer horseback riding, and the property is located on a working farm," explains Fox, who for the past few years has been listing their ranch on Airbnb and VRBO to obtain additional bookings.

"I thought I would give the short-term rental services a try, as a way to expand our business and promote it to a broader audience. I was hearing so much hype about Airbnb, for example, that I decided to try it," explains Fox. "What we offer that stands out on Airbnb is a 'secluded mountain getaway experience' that has multiple guestrooms that can accommodate couples, an entire family, or a small group of friends traveling together. In order to set it apart, I really promote within our property listing that the ranch offers a way to unplug and get away from city life."

One of the things that Fox believes her guests appreciate during their stay is the level of interaction they have each day with her and her husband. According to Fox, "I maintain a lot of interaction with our guests, starting when they book their reservation.

"I think one of the keys to ensuring people will have a good stay is to maintain a steady flow of communication. We explain what guests should expect before they arrive, so they know, for example, that there is a shared bathroom and that they'll be staying on a farm. We are not operating a five-star hotel. It's a farm. Not everything on the ground is dirt, and once in a while, you may see a fly in the house. We are open and honest about this, so people understand what to expect when they arrive and are not disappointed."

In fact, Fox seems to go out of her way to keep expectations low, making it much easier to exceed the expectations guests have upon their arrival. "I am very honest about everything. When a potential guest asks what there is to do in the area, I make it clear that there is very little to do, and people come here mainly to unplug and relax. This is very appealing to some people, but it turns out to be too quiet and too secluded for others. If someone does check in, but comes to me and explains that my property is not what they were looking for, I will always let them out of their reservation commitment, so we part ways on good terms. Based on my experience, open and honest communication with guests is always very important."

For Fox, operating a bed-and-breakfast has allowed her and her husband to earn an extra income while at the same time have the opportunity to meet interesting people from all over the world.

▶ **Fox,** continued

"We have had people stay with us from Africa, China, Korea, Italy, and many other exotic and wonderful places. Since we have been doing this for so long, we have many guests who return to visit us year after year, and in some cases, we have three generations of family members who have visited us," adds Fox.

Even though the experience that Fox is able to offer through her property is unique, she still focuses on what other hotels, motels, and B&Bs within a 20-mile radius of the ranch are charging in terms of setting her nightly rate. "We do provide breakfast every morning for our guests, but at the same time, we have shared bathrooms. Our guests have free reign of an entire house, including a common living room and dining room. My husband and I actually live in a separate house that's also located on the land. We offer to prepare breakfast every morning, but guests can use the kitchen to prepare their own meals as well. I try to accommodate whatever the guest wants," she explains.

"Because of our location, we frequently have cyclists who travel by day and stay at a different B&B each night that are along their route. I always offer to do our guest's laundry, free of charge, if they've been on the road for a while. I think one thing people enjoy is that my husband is a great storyteller, and we're just nice and welcoming people. We don't discriminate against any type of guest. We welcome everyone who wants to stay with us. I always try to make everyone feel at home," says Fox.

Prior to working with online services like Airbnb that require guests to prepay for their booking, Fox never accepted a deposit with a directly made new reservation. Fox explains, "I just trust people. On occasion, I got burned because people made a reservation, and then didn't show up. As a result, I lost the revenue from that booking and having guests stay with us on those nights. Aside from that, we've encountered very few problems or challenges. I know it sounds kind of strange, but looking back over the past 32 years, I can't think of anything I would have done differently as a host."

Fox describes her ranch as being filled with decorative and valuable antiques and cowboy memorabilia, yet she's never had a problem with a guest stealing, mishandling, or damaging anything on the property. Fox adds, "I few years back, I had a woman mail me back a washcloth that she accidently packed when she checked out. We've had so many genuinely nice people stay with us over the years that I don't worry about guests stealing or damaging our property. Most of the guests treat our property as if it's their own home and are overly cautious about

▶ **Fox,** continued

keeping everything neat and clean. I sometimes have to remind them that they're staying on a farm, and that it's OK if they have dirt on their shoes when they come inside."

As recommended by Airbnb, Fox has created a house manual that she presents to guests when they arrive. It outlines the basic rules, like no smoking in the house, and that guests must not wander off and interact with any of the animals unless they're supervised. Children are also not allowed in the swimming pool without parental supervision.

"I think my experience working as a teacher has made it very easy for me to tell people no, but to do it in a kind and respectful way," says Fox, who believes that the reviews she receives from guests are extremely important to her ongoing success as a host.

"I always keep the bathrooms and kitchen very clean, but living on a ranch, dirt gets into the house, and guests need to understand this. It's a vastly different experience from staying at a hotel in the middle of a major city. I have found that some people don't make this differentiation and will provide a lower cleanliness score when writing their review, without taking into account they stayed at a ranch and working farm. The one thing I do constantly emphasize with guests is that if they see or experience something wrong, they should bring it to my attention immediately so I can address it while the guest is still there. I also encourage constructive criticism, so I can learn how to make a guest's experience better," says Fox.

Based on her experience listing her property with short-term rental services, including www. bedandbreakfast.com, VRBO, and Airbnb, Fox has found that guests are more apt to leave a bad review if they experience something they don't like, than they are to leave a good review if they have an amazing stay.

"I would say that the biggest misconception new hosts have is that being a host is easy and offers a way to earn easy money. It's not easy. It can be a lot of work, and you're responsible for keeping your guests happy 24/7. When guests are staying at your property, you're always on duty and on call. Being a good host takes a lot of planning, coordinating, and organizational skills. Hosts also have to be tolerant and be able to interact well with all kinds of people, while always treating people with respect," says Fox.

Based on her experience, people in general are very demanding and have high expectations. "Some guests also tend to carry with them a sense of entitlement. Guests don't always understand that when they stay at an Airbnb property or at a B&B, they're not going to get

► **Fox,** continued

the same level of personalized service that they'd receive from a Hilton or Four Seasons hotel, for example. Having the ability to interact well with people is an important skill for a host to possess," she adds. "Not only do good communication skills help you maintain positive relationships with guests while they're staying with you, [they] can also result in [guest] sharing positive word-of-mouth publicity about your property. At this point, more than 60 percent of our business is from repeat customers or a direct result of a word-of-mouth referral from a past guest."

Another piece of advice that Fox has to offer new Airbnb hosts is that before they start hosting other people, they should do some traveling themselves and stay at other Airbnb properties, in order to see firsthand what the experience is like for guests and to learn more about what works and what doesn't by seeing and experiencing how other hosts perform their duties.

For example, if you happen to be cooking breakfast or preparing a pot of coffee in the morning, invite your guest to join you, and don't charge them for the food or coffee.

However, if you list additional services or amenities you have to offer within your property listing, and state an extra fee applies, you then have the opportunity to charge those applicable extra fees. For example, you might charge a per-hour rate to spend time with a guest driving them around your city (in your own car) and acting as their tour guide, allow them to rent a bicycle from you, or charge them extra for preparing them a home-cooked dinner every night.

Based on Airbnb's guidelines, if you opt to charge a guest for value-added extras, above and beyond the nightly rate to stay at your property, these fees must be described in advance and then collected via the Airbnb service. As the host, you're not supposed to accept payments directly from your guests for any extra services or amenities you provide. This is also the case with virtually all other travel hosting services.

tip

Based on your situation and what you're offering, you may discover that simply increasing your nightly rate and then providing extra services or amenities will be more acceptable to your guests, as opposed to charging them a nightly rate and then requesting additional fees for extra services/ amenities that you choose not to include for that nightly rate.

If you need to charge a guest more money, always use the Airbnb's Resolution Center www.airbnb.com/resolutions) to process these payments. Likewise, if guests want to extend their stay with you, this should be handled through the Airbnb service. As the host, you should not agree to extend guests stay (perhaps at a discounted rate), and then be paid directly in cash for the additional nights.

The Power
of Positive
Reviews

Reviews are opinions that other people rely on to make educated decisions about things like what movies to watch, what music to listen to, what products to purchase, and where they should stay when they travel. Thus, Airbnb relies heavily on a review- and rating-based system to help hosts and guest alike make intelligent choices.

Travelers can use ratings and reviews to figure out which Airbnb properties past guests have really liked and which hosts are the most hospitable, while hosts can evaluate a guest's past reviews to determine whether or not to accept a booking request.

For Airbnb and most other short-term rental services, ratings and reviews are extremely important in the decision-making process for a potential guest. Most people base their decision on several factors, including: location, price, property description, property photos, property reviews/ratings, and host reviews/ratings.

For example, if a traveler is planning to stay for a few nights in the Washington, DC, area and is looking for a private room, they'll have hundreds of options to choose from. Assuming they narrow down their selection to a handful of properties in the same price range, that are located in the same general area, and that offer the same basic amenities, the decision about where to stay will likely come down to which property and host has the best ratings and reviews.

In fact, many savvy Airbnb travelers (your potential guests) won't even consider staying at a property that doesn't have an average five-star rating, based on at least a dozen reviews, or they won't stay with a host with below a five-star rating, or who has not earned the Superhost accreditation.

Each written review is accompanied by a star-based rating. The person writing a review is asked to provide between one (worst) and five (best) stars related to a series of categories, which will be discussed shortly. These individual star-based ratings are combined into an average star-based rating, which takes into account how many reviews the average is based on. So, if a host, for example, has an overall average five-star rating based on 50 reviews, that's a lot more impressive than a host with an average three-star rating that's based on only ten reviews.

> **tip**
>
> Keep in mind, a review on Airbnb is text-based, and written by either a guest (to describe their experience staying at an Airbnb property) or a host (to describe a guest). Once a review is published on Airbnb, it can seldom be edited or deleted after 48 hours of being published, unless extenuating circumstances apply. However, if one party does not agree with the other party's review, a text-based comment or reply can be added that offers the other party's point of view.

How the Airbnb Community Utilizes Reviews

Airbnb reviews (as well as the review system offered by most other short-term rental services) are based on a specific person's opinions, which may or may not be accurate and that are highly subjective. For example, you might stay at a property and write a review that states the bathroom was spotless. However, someone else might visit that same property and write a less favorable review because they noticed the trash can in the bathroom had not been emptied recently and was bothered by that.

Thus, while every review and rating you receive is important, and should be highly favorable, your average ratings are equally important. These take into account the opinions, reviews, and ratings of multiple people. Thus, if ten different guests rate a bathroom as being less than spotless, chances are the critique has some validity.

Some travelers will invest the time to read every review a host and their property has received. Others will invest just a few seconds to take a look at the average star ratings the host and property have received when making their decision about where to stay.

Ultimately, as a host, if you have many more negative or neutral reviews than positive ones, this is going to cost you a lot of future business. Far fewer potential guests are going to risk staying with you, especially if there are numerous other Airbnb properties in the area that have earned higher reviews and better ratings, even if the nightly rate to stay at one of those properties is higher.

How Reviews Work on Airbnb

When a guest looks at an initial listing for a property, each listing displays a photo of the property, a headline, the nightly rate, the type of accommodation being offered (private room, shared room, entire house, etc.), and how many guests the property can accommodate. A thumbnail photo of the host, the average star rating the property has received (between one and five stars), and an indication of how many reviews that average rating is based upon is also provided.

As the host, you get to customize the listing for your property. You can write an attention-getting headline, offer a competitive nightly rate (that you set), and showcase an awesome-looking property photo, for example. At the same time, you can forego including a profile photo of yourself, or just write something very basic for your

tip

Earning positive host and property reviews and rating are equally important on all of the travel hosting services. Each service offers its own tools that allow guests to rate and review their hosts, as well as the properties where they stay. Prospective guests will rely heavily on these ratings and reviews, so they can ultimately make or break your ability to achieve long-term success as a travel host.

headline. Your listing, however, automatically showcases your average star-based rating and the number of reviews you've received. There's no way to hide this rating and review information.

Once you capture someone's attention with your property's search result listing, and that person clicks on that listing to view more information, it's from the property listing screen that a vast amount of information is displayed about your property. Plus, a potential guest can click or tap on your name and/or thumbnail profile photo in order to view your personal profile.

As potential guests view your full property listing, they can click on the View Photos option to see all of the images you've included with your listing. Or, they can scroll down to view all of the information that's displayed below the About This Listing heading.

This information is broken up and displayed under a series of headings, which include: The Space, Amenities, Prices, Description, House Rules, Availability, and Guestbook. Again, this is all the information you have provided and have control over. By continuing to scroll downward, another heading that's labeled [Insert Number] Reviews is displayed.

Next to this heading, the property's average star rating and the number of reviews that property has received are once again displayed. There's also a Ratings Summary chart, which offers average star ratings based on a handful of categories.

Here's a quick synopsis of what each of these highly subjective rating categories relates to:

▶ *Accuracy.* This allows someone to determine how accurate, forthcoming, and honest the host is related to their property listing, as well as the information the host shared with their guest(s) during their messaging conversations, for example.

▶ *Communication.* This is a rating based on a host's response time when communicating with a guest and whether the responses provided were accurate, helpful, and easily understandable. If a guest asks five questions as they've booked a reservation, for example, but the host responded only by answering one of the questions after a 15-hour wait, this would result in a poor communication rating.

▶ *Cleanliness.* This relates to the overall cleanliness of the property, including the bedroom(s), bathroom(s), and common areas.

▶ *Location.* This rating relates to how convenient the property's location is to local landmarks, attractions, points of interest, public transportation, nearby shopping, restaurants, bars, or whatever the guest is personally interested in. Again, this is highly subjective, based on each guest's unique interpretation of what they deem as being convenient to where their itinerary dictated they needed to be.

▶ *Check In.* This rating relates to how welcome the guest felt when they first arrived and how smoothly the initial introductions and property tour went, for example. If someone arrives at your property at the mutually agreed upon time to check in, but you are nowhere to be found, this could result is a poor check-in rating. Likewise, if you welcome the guest, but forego a tour and simply hand the guest a key, and then walk away, this too demonstrates a lack of hospitality which will typically result in a lower check-in rating.

▶ *Value.* Based on your nightly rate and what your property offers in terms of comfort, cleanliness, safety, amenities, and your hospitality, each guest is asked to rate whether or not staying with you and paying your nightly rate is a good value. For example, if you're charging a competitive nightly rate but offering a bunch of complementary amenities that go above and beyond what most Airbnb hosts offer, you'll typically receive a high value rating (five stars) from a guest for this category.

▶ List All Positive Changes and Upgrades to Your Property within Your Property Listing(s)

The month and year a review was published is displayed in conjunction with each review. So, if a review is more than six months old, chances are the host has made changes to the property and its offerings, so that older review may no longer be representative of what a future guest will actually experience. If this is the case for your property, be sure you promote this clearly in the description.

For example, if you have added a brand-new bed with a new mattress into the guestroom, promote this in your property listing's description, and state when the new bed and mattress were added.

Also, if a potential guest sends you a message (via Airbnb's messaging service) prior to requesting a booking, you can use this opportunity to mention what new amenities you're now offering.

warning

Anyone who views your property description while visiting the Airbnb website or while using the Airbnb mobile app has the ability to click or tap on the Report This Listing option, if they believe any content you've provided is false, offensive, discriminatory, or misleading, for example. Any time a listing is flagged, it will be reviewed by someone at Airbnb.

The At-a-Glance ratings chart that's displayed with each property listing gives a prospective guest a good idea about what other people have experienced staying at the selected property, particularly if the average ratings are based on dozens or hundreds of reviews from past guests.

By scrolling down further on a property listing's screen, prospective guests can read each individual text-based review that was written by a past guest, plus click on the Helpful button if they thought the review provided useful information in helping them choose a property. Anyone using the Airbnb service can click on the Helpful button when reading a review, if they believe a particular review is informative. For someone to be able to write a review, however, they must have already stayed with you as a guest.

As you'll discover, some past guests will write long and detailed reviews of their experience staying at an Airbnb property (utilizing the maximum of 500 words that's allowed). Others will write one short sentence and quickly provide the star ratings. Many guests, especially if they've had a positive experience staying with you, will forego writing a review altogether (which saves them time, but doesn't help you to build up your credibility as a host). Thus, one of your challenges will be getting your guests to actually write and publish a review and submit their ratings upon checkout.

It's important to understand that as a host, the Airbnb service also automatically tracks your performance when it comes to your response rate and response times. This information is displayed as part of your property listing, below the Your Host heading. This is another reason why responding to all incoming inquiries from potential guests in a very timely manner is so important.

tip

When a host turns on the Instant Book feature, a lightning bolt is displayed to the right of the nightly rate to indicate this. Some Airbnb travelers rely heavily on this feature because it saves them time when making a confirmed reservation once they choose where they want to stay. Airbnb also gives search result placement preference to properties that have the Instant Book feature turned on.

A Property's Location Is Important Too

Another element of each property listing is a detailed map that shows your property's location as well as other points of interest from your optional house guidebook. Upon reading your property listing, a potential guest can also click on the Similar Listings link that is included at the bottom of the screen, or click on the Request to Book button in order to make a reservation if you have the Instant Book featured turned off. When the Instant Book feature is turned on, anyone viewing your listing can instantly make a confirmed reservation by clicking or tapping on the Instant Book button.

Keep in mind, when anyone using the Airbnb service views your personal profile, they can see the number of reviews you have received and whether or not you've been verified. Also displayed on your profile page are the Reviews from Guests you've received as a host, as well as Reviews from Hosts you've received when you've traveled and stayed at other Airbnb properties as a guest.

Many savvy Airbnb travelers will look at a potential host's profile page to read all of the host's past reviews in order to learn more about them. These same people will look for the Verified badge and the Superhost badge, when evaluating you as a potential host.

warning

As a host, if you cancel a guest's confirmed reservation for a reason that Airbnb does not consider to be an extenuating circumstance, a negative review will automatically be added to your profile as what Airbnb refers to as one of the "host cancelation penalties." These reviews remain visible within your profile permanently. To learn more about host cancelation penalties, visit: www.airbnb.com/help/article/990/i-m-a-host-what-penalties-apply-if-i-need-to-cancel-a-reservation.

How Ratings Affect Becoming an Airbnb Superhost

Another feature that can be used to attract potential guests to your property listing is your ability as a host to display the Superhost emblem in conjunction with your name and profile photo. To learn more about this program, visit www.airbnb.com/superhost.

As you learned from Chapter 2, "Get Started as an Airbnb Host," the Superhost designation is something you must earn from Airbnb after becoming an experienced host, by providing "extraordinary experiences for your guests." Once a host earns this designation, Airbnb reevaluates it four times per year to ensure that the host has maintained the level of standards required to be called a Superhost.

tip

Especially when you get along really well with your guests, exchange email addresses and/or social media details, and then follow up with your guest with a thank-you note one day after their check out. Ask if they made it home safely, thank them for staying with you, and politely remind them to write a review about their experience. Of course, you should also invite them to stay with you again in the future and mention that they should feel free to tell their friends about their positive experience staying with you.

In a nutshell, to become a Superhost, you must have maintained a good standing account on the Airbnb service for the previous 12-month period, plus have hosted at least ten trips, maintained a 90 percent response rate or better, at least 80 percent of your ratings must be five-stars (provided at least half of the guests who have stayed with you publish a review), and you must complete each confirmed reservation without cancelations.

You can learn more about these requirements by visiting www.airbnb.com/help/article/829/how-do-i-become-a-superhost. As a host, you do not need to apply for the Superhost designation. Airbnb automatically keeps track of your performance. If and when you meet the appropriate criteria, you will be awarded Superhost status. Until you achieve this status, you can determine how far along you are toward earning it by viewing the Superhost section of the Dashboard any time after you become an active host.

Once you become a Superhost, you're automatically given extra benefits by Airbnb. For example, you receive "priority phone support" when you call Airbnb or tweet them a question (via Twitter) by addressing it to @Airbnbhelp. In addition, your property listing is more apt to be seen by potential guests, because the Airbnb service offers a search filter option that allows travelers to view Superhost properties exclusively, once they select a destination.

If you earn the Superhost status and are able to maintain it for one year, which is equivalent to four evaluation periods, you automatically receive a $100 travel coupon to use when you travel and stay as a guest at another Airbnb property. Plus, as a Superhost, you'll be invited to attend special events and preview new Airbnb features before other hosts.

tip

To read the most up-to-date terms and conditions a host must adhere to in order to receive and then keep the Superhost designation, visit: www.airbnb.com/superhost/terms.

Ten Tips for Generating the Best Possible Reviews from Guests

The following are ten tips that will help to ensure you earn the best possible reviews from your guests. These tips recap some of the core and most important concepts that have been discussed elsewhere in this book.

1. Respond to booking requests, questions, and concerns from potential guests as quickly as possible.

▶ Word-of-Mouth Referrals Are Equally Important

Within the Airbnb community (or any short-term rental service's community), as a host, striving to earn the best reviews and five-star ratings is a worthwhile endeavor that will significantly enhance your credibility and reputation. Just as important, however, is meeting or exceeding your guests' expectations so that they're inclined to tell their friends, family, and others about their experience. Ideally, you want all of your past guests to recommend your property to people they know and provide a specific referral to your Airbnb property listing.

Just as hotels, B&Bs, and all other businesses rely on word-of-mouth referrals to increase their business, as an Airbnb host, you can also use them to work in your favor. After all, wouldn't you prefer a potential guest who is looking to stay in your geographic area to sign into the Airbnb service and specifically seek out your property listing, as opposed to browsing through dozens or hundreds of other listings before stumbling upon yours?

While a guest is staying with you, if they tell you how much they're enjoying their stay, thank them for the kind words, and simply respond by telling them to tell their friends. If a guest chooses to share details about their stay with you on social media, for example, ask them to include a direct link to your Airbnb property listing within their post. This allows people to click on that link and be forwarded directly to your property listing.

Your unique property listing web page address (URL) can be found by signing into the Airbnb service and viewing your listing as a traveler. When viewing the listing, copy the URL from the address field of your web browser. It will look something like this: www.airbnb.com/rooms/########. The "#"s represent your unique listing number within the Airbnb system. You can remove any additional information within the URL that's displayed after this unique number.

2. Be honest when creating your property listing and personal profile.

3. Offer something unique that other nearby Airbnb properties don't offer, or make a point to offer a great value based on your nightly rate.

4. Set up House Rules that get everyone on the same page in terms of what guests can and can't do while staying at your property.

5. Provide a clean, safe, and comfortable environment for your guests.

6. Welcome your guests personally when they arrive, and then be on hand for their checkout.

7. Provide extra amenities, on a complimentary basis, that will make a guest more comfortable.

8. Create a clearly written and easy to understand home manual.

9. Check in with your guests periodically during their stay.

10. Always be polite and professional when interacting with potential and actual guests. Try to avoid allowing small disagreements or misunderstandings to escalate into formal complaints that get submitted to Airbnb.

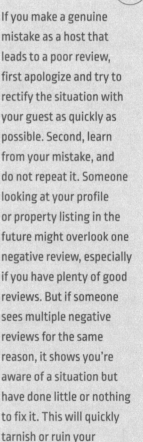

warning

If you make a genuine mistake as a host that leads to a poor review, first apologize and try to rectify the situation with your guest as quickly as possible. Second, learn from your mistake, and do not repeat it. Someone looking at your profile or property listing in the future might overlook one negative review, especially if you have plenty of good reviews. But if someone sees multiple negative reviews for the same reason, it shows you're aware of a situation but have done little or nothing to fix it. This will quickly tarnish or ruin your reputation and credibility as a host.

Responding to Negative Reviews

If, as a host, you receive a bad review from a guest, it's important to consider the following:

▶ You might have done something wrong as a host that resulted in you and your property not meeting or exceeding the expectations of your guest. For example, perhaps your property listing or information within your profile was misleading, badly worded, or created expectations within the guest's mind that their experience staying with you didn't live up to.

▶ As a host, perhaps you said or did something to anger or offend your guest.

▶ One or more things within your property didn't work or caused your guest discomfort.

▶ You did not achieve your objective of providing a clean, comfortable, and safe place to stay at a reasonable price.

To avoid receiving similar negative reviews in the future, based on what the negative review says, seriously consider what you could have done to rectify the situation while the guest was still staying with you. Next, fix whatever is wrong before your next guest checks in.

Remember, you have 48 hours after a review is published to make contact with the guest and try to rectify the situation, apologize, or reach an understanding or arrangement that will result in the guest modifying their review before it becomes permanently linked with your profile or property listing. Under no circumstances, however, should you ever threaten a guest, try to extort a good review, or do anything that goes against any of Airbnb's policies and guidelines.

Assuming a negative review does wind up being posted, you have 14 days to add a public response to that review. Unfortunately, this public response has no impact on the star ratings the former guest included with their review. It simply allows you to share your point of view, or your side of the story, in hopes of reducing the impact the negative review has on your reputation as a host.

Airbnb's Policies and Guidelines Are Constantly Evolving

It's important to understand that Airbnb continuously strives to provide the best possible community experience for all of its travelers and hosts. Part of this commitment involves the need to occasionally adapt its policies and guidelines to meet current demands and trends in our global society.

Earlier in this chapter, we provided web page links that allow you to review Airbnb's up-to-date Content Policy and Review Guidelines. We also provided links to Airbnb's Extortion Policy, Standards & Expectations, and Nondiscrimination Policies in previous chapters. To find links for all of these documents, visit www.airbnb.com/help/topic/250/terms-policies.

As a host, it's important that you periodically review each of these documents, so you stay up to date on new or revised policies that govern how you host your guests, and what behaviors and actions are acceptable. Airbnb has made it clear that, moving forward, it will be enforcing its policies in a much stricter way.

For example, on September 8, 2016, Brian Chesky, the CEO and cofounder of Airbnb, sent an email to all community members. Within the email, he stated, "Discrimination is the opposite of belonging, and its existence on our platform jeopardizes this core mission. Bias and discrimination have no place on Airbnb, and we have zero tolerance for them. Unfortunately, we have been slow to address these problems, and for this I am sorry. I take responsibility for any pain or frustration this has caused members of our community. We will not only make this right; we will work to set an example that other companies can follow."

Starting November 1, 2016, everyone who uses Airbnb was asked to agree to a revised and more detailed anti-discrimination policy, which became an integral piece of what Airbnb now refers to as its Community Commitment.

Part of this Community Commitment policy states, "We believe that no matter who you are, where you are from, or where you travel, you should be able to belong in the Airbnb community. By joining this community, you commit to treat all fellow members of this community, regardless of race, religion, national origin, disability, sex, gender identity, sexual orientation or age, with respect, and without judgment or bias."

If you are unwilling or unable to follow these polices as an Airbnb host, don't bother becoming one, because this revenue-generating opportunity and the Airbnb community is not for you.

How to Write Reviews About Your Guests

According to Airbnb's Review Guidelines, as a host reviewing a recent guest, you're asked to "stick to the facts" and provide useful information to the people who will be reading the review.

Each review should simply describe your personal experience related to a guest or reservation. It can't be used to endorse or promote any harmful or illegal activity or include any type of general social commentary.

You're also not allowed to use a review in order to violate another person's rights, or include content that is being used for extortion, that relates to an Airbnb

aha!

Just as it's optional for guests to write a review about their host and the Airbnb property they stayed at, it's optional for hosts to write a review about each of their guests. Especially if you had a problem with a guest, writing a review will help other Airbnb hosts potentially avoid that same problem by declining that guest's booking request in the future. The time you invest writing reviews of your guests helps the Airbnb community as a whole. However, if you have something really nice to say about a guest, and you publish a review on Airbnb, this might further encourage that guest to write a review about their experience staying with you, so you benefit as well.

▶ Meet Airbnb Host Andrew Kamphey

According to Andrew Kamphey, he is an avid world traveler. Almost a decade ago, he learned about CouchSurfing.com, and since then both hosted other travelers in his home and stayed in strangers' homes for free during his own travels.

"This experience got me comfortable with the idea that I could share my living space with other people. So, when Airbnb came along, it provided a logical next step that would allow me to earn money from hosting people who stayed in my apartment. My experience thus far as an Airbnb host has helped me pay my rent, meet new people, and create lasting friendships," says Kamphey.

"In addition, for my work, I am occasionally asked to travel. I asked my superiors if I could find less costly accommodations using Airbnb, versus staying at a hotel that the employer was already willing to pay for, if I could keep the difference. They agreed, and this allowed me to earn extra money when I traveled for work," adds Kamphey, who has since met numerous other business travelers who have utilized this strategy.

Once Kamphey settled down into his own one-bedroom apartment in Los Angeles after all of his global traveling he almost immediately decided to become an Airbnb host. Now, whenever he travels for business or leisure, he uses Airbnb to rent out his Los Angeles apartment. "Based on the money I earn from Airbnb renting out my apartment for two weeks out of the month, for example, I am able to pay my full month's rent, so in essence, I live at my apartment rent-free when I am there," explains Kamphey.

Because Kamphey is not always available to welcome his guests, he worked out a deal with his good friend, who lives locally, to serve as his representative when in-person interaction with guests is required. In addition, one of his neighbors operates a maid service, so he hired his neighbor to help maintain the apartment and keep it clean in between guests. Kamphey adds, "As a result, my good friend makes some money, my neighbor is profiting, I earn some extra money, and my rent is covered, all thanks to Airbnb."

Kamphey also explains that Airbnb has given him an incentive to travel. Because much of his work as a social media consultant can be done remotely, if someone wants to rent his apartment through Airbnb while he was otherwise planning to be home, he uses this an excuse to take an impromptu trip.

"I have wound up leaving town and heading to places like Las Vegas, Tijuana, as well as Santa Barbara, Oakland, and Ventura, California, where I visited with friends, for example," he adds.

▶ **Kamphey,** continued

"This travel was made possible from the income I earned from Airbnb. I love the added income that being an Airbnb host provides, and the freedom it's given me to do more of my own traveling."

Among the first things that Kamphey did when he decided to become an Airbnb host was seek out the guidance of a close friend who was already a successful Airbnb host. "She provided some tips when I was creating my property listing on Airbnb and offered advice on setting my nightly rate. She recommended that I utilize the Smart Pricing feature to help maximize my revenue," says Kamphey.

"One lesson I learned early on was the need to charge a fair price based on what is actually being offered and what other accommodation options are charging nearby. After hosting one of my first guests, I received an unfavorable rating related to value, because it turns out I was charging slightly too much for what I was offering, compared to what nearby Airbnb hosts were charging for similar accommodations. The guest's expectations were set too high for the value I was offering. I quickly adjusted my nightly pricing to adapt better to local demand and nearby competition," adds Kamphey.

Within his one-bedroom apartment that he rents out through Airbnb, Kamphey offers a selection of popular board games for his guests to play. He explains, "I have found that many of my guests wind up having down time while staying at the apartment, and having board games on hand allows them to relax and be entertained. Many of my guests have family and friends in the area, and my guests tend to invite those people to the apartment to socialize. The board games provide an opportunity for people to hang out with their friends, as opposed to walking to a nearby bar, for example. I think the games compensate for the fact that the apartment does not have a television set or entertainment center within it.

"One of the amenities that guests tend to ask for is a television with cable programming. I plan to add this shortly in order to accommodate this demand. In comparison to a hotel, my apartment offers more space than a traditional hotel room and is less expensive per night.

"I have found that honesty is always a good policy when dealing with guests. There was one instance where construction was being done near my apartment and it was very loud. I already had a guest booked to stay here, but I thought they'd be very disappointed with the noise. I told them about the problem before they arrived, and they agreed it would be fine. Since they expected the noise, they did not complain or leave a bad review," says Kamphey. "I did have one

▶ **Kamphey,** continued

negative rating from a different guest early on, because someone felt the shower curtain was dirty. This is why it's particularly important to offer a clean and spotless bathroom."

Like so many other hosts, Kamphey discovered than even if you offer an in-depth tour of the property when someone checks in, and you show them how to work the appliances and shower, for example, within two hours, they forget what you said. He says, "My house manual comprises one sheet of paper, and it outlines how to work everything in the apartment, and it provides a listing of grocery stores, restaurants, and bars that are walking distance from the apartment."

Because Kamphey received negative reviews early on in his Airbnb hosting career, he now spends a little more time interacting with guests before they arrive in order to avoid the same misunderstandings that lead to the negative feedback he received in the past.

"I ask more questions. For example, if I learn someone will not have access to a car, they need to understand that my apartment is a good 20-minute walk to the closest grocery store, restaurant or movie theater, because the apartment is located in a very residential community. When people tell me why they're coming into town, and what they plan to do during their stay, I can easily determine if my apartment will provide adequate accommodations," explains Kamphey.

He adds, "Reviews and ratings on Airbnb that hosts receive from guests turn out to be very important. If you receive ratings that are less than five stars, multiple times in a row, you are going to hear from Airbnb and will likely need to fix the issues that people are complaining about, even if the issues are very minor. Having good reviews and becoming a Superhost, for example, gets you better positioning in Airbnb search results, which means more people are apt to see your listing.

"Learn as much as you can from your ratings and reviews, and make adjustments to your property and your hosting practices, based on the constructive criticisms and feedback you receive. One way to avoid misunderstandings is to create and share a detailed list of house rules and outline what is expected of your guests. This is definitely something I needed to spend more time doing early on when I first became an Airbnb host."

Based on his firsthand experience, Kamphey has learned the importance of being flexible and patient with his guests and recommends that other hosts also develop these skills. "Understand that people's travel plans change, or they encounter unavoidable delays. As a host, you need

► **Kamphey,** continued

to be understanding and able to deal with this," he says. "This is particularly important when people arrive and check in for the first time. Also, have backup plans in place in case something goes wrong and you're not available to address or fix the situation in person. Have spare keys available with your neighbors, or have someone else who you trust and who lives and works nearby on hand to provide backup as your representative whenever you're not available."

investigation, or that is in any way harmful, threatening, obscene, profane, vulgar, discriminatory, or defamatory. All content within your review must also adhere to Airbnb's Content Policy, which you can learn more about here: www.airbnb.com/help/article/546/ what-is-airbnb-s-content-policy.

The following are some host guidelines to keep in mind when writing a review about a recent guest:

► You have up to 14 days after a guest checks out to write and publish your review. Once published, the reviews remain online and visible indefinitely.

► A review can contain up to 500 words, and must follow Airbnb's Review Guidelines, which are at www.airbnb.com/help/article/13/how-do-reviews-work.

► A review of a guest can be edited for up to 48 hours after it's published online, or until that guest completes and publishes their own review of you and your property. After that time, only reviews that violate Airbnb's Review Guidelines will be removed from the service by Airbnb.

► Once a review has been published it remains online indefinitely. It can't be deleted. It's possible for either party to write a public response that will be displayed along with the review. However, a response must be posted within 14 days after the initial review has been published.

Managing Finances for an Airbnb Hosting Business

M any people decide to become an Airbnb host for the social interaction and the opportunity to make new friends. Others use this as a way to help offset their monthly living expenses, or as a way to generate extra income that can be used to improve their lifestyle. The thing to remember, however, is that once you become an Airbnb host and begin inviting paying guests into your home or property, you immediately become a business operator.

Thus, you need to handle your finances like a businessperson. Some of the additional responsibilities this entails include:

aha!

To help you understand Airbnb's current payout fees and policies, visit www.airbnb.com/help/ article/459/how-do-i-calculate-my-payout. Keep in mind, your payout can be affected by whether you charge a cleaning or other type of fee and whether you activate a special offer or extended-stay discount to your guests. The breakdown of your earnings for each separate booking/reservation is displayed when you visit the Transaction History tool that's offered by Airbnb.

▶ Understanding the fees associated with being an Airbnb host (or a host with any short-term rental service). For example, for every guest booking that's processed through Airbnb, you're charged a 3-percent host service fee every time a reservation is completed. This fee is calculated based on the reservation subtotal, prior to other fees and taxes which apply to the reservation. When applicable within the European Union, calculated into the host service fee may be a VAT (Value Added Tax), based on where you live and local laws.

▶ Choosing how Airbnb will transfer money to you via its Payout Preferences tools. For example, providing your bank account or PayPal account details, as required.

▶ Maintaining accurate and up-to-date financial records. Consider using bookkeeping (accounting) software such as Intuit's QuickBooks or QuickBooks for Rental Properties, plus keeping organized, paper-based or scanned files related to all financial records and receipts from short-term rental-related purchases and expenses. Depending on your needs, the online-edition of QuickBooks may be a less costly option to use.

▶ Adhering to all local, state, and federal rules that apply to short-term renting your property (with the understanding that these ordinances, laws, and regulations are subject to change at any time in the future).

▶ Acquiring and maintaining a business license or permit, as required by your local government.

▶ Adhering to the rules outlined by your homeowner's association, co-op board, or apartment lease that pertain to using your house, condo, or apartment for short-term rentals.

▶ Calculating and paying local, state, and federal taxes that apply to you personally, as well as your travel hosting business.

▶ Working with an accountant (CPA) to help you set up and manage the financial bookkeeping associated with your travel hosting business.

▶ Managing your additional and ongoing travel-hosting-related expenses, so that they don't exceed your profits.

▶ Understanding how to access and utilize the financial reporting tools provided by Airbnb, including the Transaction History information, which reports what you've earned and when you've earned it, as well as your gross earnings.

▶ Adhering to all of Airbnb's policies and guidelines (www.airbnb.com/help/topic/250/terms-policies), which are periodically updated.

Some of these tasks and added responsibilities may seem daunting at first. Once you understand what needs to be accomplished based on your personal situation, you can work with professionals—for example, an accountant, professional bookkeeper, or lawyer—to help you set everything up correctly right from the start and learn how to maintain the proper financial records.

Understand how your bookkeeping and tax responsibilities will change once you become a travel host. Researching what local, state, and federal laws, ordinances, and regulations you may need to adhere to will require some effort on your part. Some of this will depend on the type of property you own, lease, or rent, where you live, and your current financial and employment situation, for example.

Once you get all of these business and financial responsibilities met, focus on becoming the best possible Airbnb host (or a host with whichever short-term rental services you opt to work with).

Calculating Your Expenses

In addition to Airbnb's imposed host service fee and your tax-related obligations, becoming an Airbnb host will require that you cover a handful of one-time and

aha!

QuickBooks from Intuit (www.quickbooks.com) is the world's most popular bookkeeping and accounting software. Various versions of QuickBooks are available as Windows PC or Mac software applications. There's also an online version of QuickBooks that works with all internet-connected computers and mobile devices. Because several different versions of QuickBooks are available, consult with your accountant and/or Intuit in order to determine which version is best suited to meet your unique needs as a travel host.

▶ Understand Your Tax Obligations

Depending on where you live, in addition to paying income taxes on your earning (when applicable), you may be responsible for paying a value-added tax (VAT), local tax, U.S. federal tax, and/or sales tax (for certain types of additional fees you charge to your guests). VATs apply to hosts based within the European Union, for example.

The following Airbnb web page describes how some of these taxes work: www.airbnb.com/help/article/481/how-do-taxes-work-for-hosts. Rather than relying solely on the information provided by Airbnb, your best strategy is to consult with an accountant who understands the short-term rental business and the tax regulations in your town, city, state, or country (if you're outside of the United States).

For example, if you determine that you need to collect a tax from your guests, this fee can be added with a Special Fee through the Airbnb service. It is your responsibility to inform potential guests of the tax amount they're being charged prior to their booking a reservation. If you're based in certain areas, the Airbnb service automatically offers a Collect and Remit feature. This helps hosts collect and pay region-specific occupancy taxes, when applicable.

Keep in mind, the Airbnb service does not handle any of the tasks associated with preparing state or federal tax returns if you're within the United States. Meeting these obligations is entirely the responsibility of the host, and failure to do so could lead to significant fines and/or legal problems.

recurring expenses so that you can provide clean, comfortable, and safe accommodations for your paying guests.

Refer to the following figures to help you identify, calculate, track, and manage these various expenses:

- ▶ *One-Time Expenses* Figure 8–1 (page 128). This worksheet will help you take inventory of what furniture and amenities you already have within your property and determine what additional one-time purchases will be required to adequately host your guests. While some of the items listed within Figure 8.1 are mandatory, others are optional, which you can acquire right away, or wait until you've begun generating revenue as an Airbnb host before making the additional financial investment.
- ▶ *Weekly or Monthly Expenses* Figure 8–2 (page 129). These are expenses you'll need to pay on a weekly or monthly basis in order to maintain your property and keep it clean, for example. Some of these expenses you may already be paying, while others

may be new once you start having guests stay with you.

▶ *Occasional Recurring Expenses* Figure 8–3 (page 130). These are expenses that you'll incur every few months, or once or twice per year. For example, while a bed frame and box spring could easily last for many years, the sheets, pillows, and blankets may need to be replaced every few months.

▶ *Frequently Recurring Expenses and Purchases* Figure 8–4 (page 131). These are expenses that you'll incur often and can relate to items you and your guests will use up and that will need to be replenished or replaced, such as toilet paper, paper towels, soap, coffee, bottled water, or shampoo. To save money, consider buying these items in bulk.

Based on how you'll be handling your financial record keeping and bookkeeping, you may find it easier and more convenient to use bookkeeping software (such as Intuit's QuickBooks) to track all of this information. If you're savvy using a spreadsheet application, such as Microsoft Excel or Apple's Numbers, you can create a custom spreadsheet to help organize and manage the financial aspects of your travel hosting business.

Additional Information About Setting Your Nightly Rate

By now, you should realize that many factors should be considered when setting your nightly rate. Strategies for setting a fair nightly rate have already been covered, but they do factor into your budget so let's quickly review some key points. As an Airbnb host, the primary way you'll generate income is by charging a nightly rate for guests to stay at your property. You already know that Airbnb (and most services like it) allow you to set your own nightly rate. To help

tip

A sheet set should include an appropriately sized fitted bed sheet, flat bed sheet, and at least two pillow cases. Be sure to have an ample supply of sets on hand for each bed, because you may need to provide clean bedding multiple times per week based on guest turnover. Plus, you should always have one or two extra sets on hand for unexpected needs. The number of sets you will need to buy and keep on hand will depend on how many beds are within your property, how often you plan to offer clean bedding to long-term guests, do laundry, and anticipate new guests.

For example, if you have one bedroom that you rent out to different guests five to seven nights per week, this will require that you have at least eight to ten sheets sets on hand, especially if you only plan to do laundry once per week.

One-Time Expenses

Description	Number Required	Already Acquired	Need to Purchase	Cost Each	Total Cost
Area Rug(s)				$	$
Bed Frame & Box Spring—King				$	$
Bed Frame & Box Spring—Twin				$	$
Bed Frame & Box Spring—Queen				$	$
Bedroom Door Lock(s)				$	$
Carbon Monoxide Detector(s)				$	$
Closet Hangers				$	$
Coffee Maker				$	$
Comforters (One per bed)				$	$
Couch & Living Room Furniture Set				$	$
Curtains/Window Shades				$	$
Desk				$	$
Desk Chair				$	$
Dining Room/Kitchen Furniture (Tables, chairs, etc.)				$	$
Dresser				$	$
Extra House Keys				$	$
Fans/Air Conditioners/Heaters				$	$
Fire Extinguisher(s)				$	$
First-Aid Kit				$	$
Guestroom Television Set & TV Stand				$	$
Home Security System				$	$
Iron & Ironing Board				$	$
Keyless-Entry Door Lock—Main Entrance				$	$
Lamps / Lighting Fixtures				$	$
Laundry Hamper(s)				$	$
Livingroom Television/Entertainment Center				$	$
Mattress—King				$	$
Mattress—Queen				$	$
Mattress—Twin				$	$

FIGURE 8–1: **One-Time Expenses**

One-Time Expenses

Description	Number Required	Already Acquired	Need to Purchase	Cost Each	Total Cost
Mirrors				$	$
Night Stand(s)				$	$
Power Strips for Guestroom(s)				$	$
Smoke Detector(s)				$	$
Trash Cans				$	$
Other:				$	$
Other:				$	$
Other:				$	$

FIGURE 8–1: **One-Time Expenses,** continued

Weekly or Monthly Expenses

Description	Payment Frequency	Total Cost
Additional Parking Pass		$
Cable TV		$
Homeowner's Association or Coop Dues		$
Homeowner's/Renter's Insurance		$
Internet (Wifi)		$
Local/State Permit		$
Phone		$
Professional Cleaning Service		$
Rent/Mortgage Payment		$
Short-Term Rental Insurance		$
Utilities—Electricity		$
Utilities—Gas		$
Other:		$
Other:		$
Other:		$

FIGURE 8–2: **Weekly or Monthly Expenses**

Occasional Recurring Expenses

Description	Number Required	How Often Purchase Is Required	Purchase Date	Cost Each	Total Cost
Bath Mat(s)				$	$
Blankets				$	$
Comforter Cover (Washable)				$	$
Home and Kitchen Appliance Maintenance & Repair				$	$
Kitchen Supplies—Dishes, Glasses, Utensils, etc.				$	$
New Towel Sets (Bath Towel, Hand Towel, Washcloth)				$	$
Pillows				$	$
Plastic Mattress Cover—King				$	$
Plastic Mattress Cover—Queen				$	$
Plastic Mattress Cover—Twin				$	$
Sheet Sets—King				$	$
Sheet Sets—Twin				$	$
Sheet Sets—Queen				$	$
Shower Curtain				$	$
Other:				$	$
Other:				$	$
Other:				$	$

FIGURE 8–3: **Occasional Recurring Expenses**

Frequently Recurring Expenses and Purchases

Description	Number Required	How Often Purchase Is Required	Cost Each	Total Cost
Bottled Water—24 Pack			$	$
Cleaning Supplies			$	$
Coffee			$	$
Dishwasher Detergent			$	$
Garbage Bags			$	$
Hand Soap			$	$
Laundry Detergent			$	$
Light Bulbs			$	$
Paper Towels			$	$
Replacement Batteries			$	$
Tissues			$	$
Toilet Paper—12 Pack			$	$
Travel-Size Toiletries Sets (Shampoo, Conditioner, Soap, etc.)			$	$
Other:			$	$
Other:			$	$
Other:			$	$

FIGURE 8–4: **Frequently Recurring Expenses and Purchases**

▶ More Considerations When Setting Your Nightly Rate

Start by setting a base nightly rate. This is the minimum nightly fee you plan to charge, regardless of other circumstances. This rate should cover your costs and allow you to earn a profit. Once this base nightly rate is set, you can increase it based on demand and other factors.

If there's a major event (concert, sporting event, conference, or convention) coming to your area that will be attracting many more travelers into the region than normal, this is an opportunity for you to charge a higher nightly rate. The local hotels, motels, and B&Bs, for example, will likely be full, but additional travelers will still need accommodations.

Every city has a visitors and conventions bureau that can provide a listing of major events scheduled to be held in your area. You should also check the event calendars at concert venues, sports arenas, convention centers, and fairgrounds within a 25-mile radius, in order to determine what major events will be taking place in the weeks and months to come.

offset your property cleaning and maintenance costs, you're also able to charge an additional cleaning fee, for example. Plus, based on other circumstances, you're able to charge extra guest fees for specific things, or offer a discount to your guests who book a long-term stay, for example.

To recap, the nightly rate you charge should be based on the following:

- ▶ The type of accommodations you're offering (shared guestroom, private guestroom, or an entire apartment or house, for example)
- ▶ The collection of included amenities and value-added services you're offering on a complimentary basis
- ▶ Your geographic location and safety of the neighborhood, in addition to its appeal for tourists or visitors
- ▶ What nearby hotels, motels, and other Airbnb hosts are charging
- ▶ Local demand (and seasonal demand)

tip

As a host, you're able to change your nightly rate at any time. (Rate changes will apply to all new reservations, not existing ones.) You're also able to manually set a different nightly rate for weeknights versus weekend nights (and/or holiday nights), or utilize Airbnb's Smart Pricing tool, which allows you to provide a nightly price range, and allows Airbnb to actually set your nightly rate(s) based on local demand and other factors.

Obviously, the nightly rate you opt to charge needs to cover the Airbnb host services fees you're required to pay, income taxes and other taxes you're responsible for, and the other expenses you'll incur as an Airbnb host. Plus, it should allow you to generate a profit (above and beyond these expenses).

Guests won't be willing to pay a nightly fee to stay at your property that's higher than what it would cost them to stay at a nearby hotel, motel, or B&B, for example. Likewise, they won't pay a rate that's not competitive with another nearby Airbnb property that offers similar accommodations and amenities but for a lower nightly fee, especially if you're competing to offer budget accommodations.

However, if your Airbnb property offers something truly unique, such as an upscale and premium location, posh furnishings, and luxury comfort, and/or you're including a collection of high-end amenities, then you may be able to charge a much higher nightly rate that your guests will be happy to pay. It will be your responsibility as the host, however, to clearly communicate what's unique or special about your property within your property listing, in a way that entices guests to want to stay with you and pay a premium rate.

Learning how to set the ideal nightly rate that covers your costs, allows you to generate profit, and that will be acceptable by your guests is a skill in itself, and one that gets easier with research and experience. Chances are, based on what you're offering, local demand (including midweek, weekend, holiday or special event demand), and your location, it will take you time and some experimentation to determine the ideal nightly rate to charge.

Independent Tools to Help You Generate the Highest Revenue Possible as a Travel Host

There are a variety of optional, online-based services you can rely on to help you enhance your hosting skills and manage your ongoing responsibilities. Some of these services provide you with proprietary research and tools, and some actually handle all aspects of setting and continuously updating your nightly rate for you, for example. Many of these optional services for travel hosts work with Airbnb as well as other travel hosting services.

▶ *Beyond Pricing* (*https://beyondpricing.com*). This site utilizes a data-driving pricing tool to help Airbnb hosts almost immediately increase their revenue by 10 to 40 percent. Once you turn on the Automated Pricing tool, the service will update your pricing daily, based on localized demand. The service currently works within hundreds of major U.S. cities, as well as in major cities throughout much of Europe, Canada, Mexico, Central America, Australia, the Middle East, and South America.

Subscribers to this service are charged a flat 1 percent of their Airbnb booking revenue.

► *Everbooked (www.everbooked.com).* This site is another online service that provides market analytics, automatic pricing tools, and competitive data to help you maximize your travel hosting profits. Currently, this service provides valuable information for Airbnb hosts with properties in more than 3,000 U.S. cities. After the free 30-day trial period, this service charges Airbnb travel hosts $20.00 per month, plus 0.75 percent of your gross booking revenues. The Everbooked Pro service charges $100.00 per month, plus 0.65 percent if your gross booking revenues.

► *Wheelhouse (www.usewheelhouse.com).* This site is an independent online service that supports Airbnb, HomeAway, and TripAdvisor travel hosts. It offers a collection of up-to-date, localized market research, as well as online interactive tools that will quickly help you set your nightly rate and potentially generate up to 40 percent higher revenue as a travel host. Some of Wheelhouse's services are free, while others require you pay a monthly subscription fee to access them. If you opt to use the Wheelhouse Smart Pricing tool to automatically set and adjust your nightly rate on an ongoing basis, for example, the service charges 1 percent of all booked nights that utilized the tool.

tip

Determine if you'd like to offer budget accommodations that might be equivalent to what a two- or three-star-rated hotel or motel would provide (and then set your nightly rate accordingly). However, if you'd like to cater to a more upscale and affluent audience and provide accommodations along the lines of what a four- or five-star-rated hotel, resort, or B&B would offer (and charge a premium nightly rate), this will require you meet or exceed the much higher expectations of these guests.

tip

Additional, independently operated, online pricing tool services available to Airbnb hosts, include PriceLabs (www.pricelabs.co), SmartHost (http://smarthost.me), and Brite Yield (http://briteyield.com). Some of these services also support travel hosts working with VRBO, FlipKey, and HomeAway, for example.

Reasons to Reinvest Profits in Your Airbnb Hosting Business

You've read how important it is for a host to offer clean, comfortable, and safe accommodations for their guests.

Assuming you do this, you'll be able to charge a nightly fee that's comparable with what other nearby Airbnb hosts charge with similar properties and amenities. Offering competitive pricing will typically earn favorable ratings and reviews from your guests, assuming your hospitality is also up to par.

Over time, however, you can improve upon your property by upgrading it with more luxurious furnishings, décor, and amenities and then potentially charge a higher nightly rate that your guests will likely be willing to pay. This becomes much easier if you've already earned a collection of excellent reviews and five-star ratings, which gives you added credibility as a host.

While you can upgrade the furnishings and décor based on your personal taste, and what you think your future guests will like, take into account the feedback you've received from past guests and your own experience as a traveler staying with other hosts to help you select the collection of amenities, décor updates, and new furnishings you'd like to offer.

Choose amenities that will be considered valuable or useful to the majority of your guests, who will appreciate them, and potentially be willing to pay a higher nightly rate to utilize them. After being an Airbnb host for an extended period, you'll develop a good understanding of the types of guests that most often stay with you, as well as what they like and don't

warning

While some of these independently operated pricing tools charge a flat monthly subscription rate, most charge a percentage of your booking revenue that's generated using the service's proprietary pricing tools. This fee is in addition to the 3 percent host service fee you're already paying to Airbnb, for example. Most of these services offer a free 30-day trial and boast using them will increase your short-term rental revenue between 10 and 40 percent. Take advantage of the free trial that's offered before making any financial commitments to any of these services.

like about your property and what you're offering. This is firsthand market research you can use to help you make intelligent decisions when it comes to upgrading your property and enhancing the collection of included amenities and/or furnishings you'll be offering.

Depending on how often you host guests, how often you will need to perform significant (and potentially costly) maintenance and upkeep on your property and its major appliances will vary. However, these are future expenses you'll need to consider if you want to continue offering clean, comfortable, and safe accommodations for your guest over time.

warning

If you're planning to sell your property sometime in the next few years, consider the impact (wear and tear) having paying guests (either periodically or continuously) will have on the property itself. Calculate how this will impact your property's resale value, especially if you don't handle ongoing maintenance in a proper and responsible manner.

Thus, long-term financial planning is required to ensure you'll have the funds on hand that are needed to pay for the timely maintenance, repair, and upkeep on the property, its furnishings, décor, and appliances.

For example, if a guest stays at your property three years from now and discovers a mattress is worn out, blankets smell moldy and have holes, the couch has tears in the upholstery, and the carpeting is ragged and stained, you'll begin earning poor ratings and reviews for not maintaining the property.

Chances are, you'll need to repaint the walls every few years, replace the carpeting every few years, pay for the repair and upkeep of the appliances, and cover a variety of other upkeep expenses that are a direct result of having many guests utilizing your property. These are all long-term or future costs you'll likely need to consider.

Unfortunately, not all of your guests will treat your property like it's their own, which will likely result in quicker wear and tear. You need to plan for this.

Consider your long-term goals and objectives. Do you want to reinvest your profits as an Airbnb host into the property in order to ultimately be able to charge a higher nightly rate and/or increase the resale value of the property when you're ready to sell it? Or, do you want to take the money you earn and use it to improve your lifestyle, pay off debts, or perhaps go on more extravagant vacations? These are among the financial decisions you'll need to make early on, once you begin your travel hosting business.

warning

Purchasing additional homes, apartments, or condos, for example, with the sole intent of using them as short-term rental properties is a viable business. However, if local or state laws or regulations change and prevent short-term rentals in the future, you'll need to have a backup plan in place in order to protect your investments. Choose additional properties wisely, and if applicable, make sure you fully understand the homeowner's association or coop bylaws and rules that pertain to short-term rentals, before investing in the property.

Make Being a Travel Host Your Full-Time Career

A small percentage of travel hosts have discovered ways to generate enough revenue to quit their full-time job and have their travel hosting business become their primary source of income. For the majority of these people, they've acquired and are managing multiple short-term rental properties. Obviously, this requires a much higher initial financial and time commitment, but it's certainly a viable opportunity as long as the properties are in areas that permit short-term rentals.

9

Other Related Services You Should Be Aware Of

The short-term rental concept has become a widely accepted way for travelers to find affordable and alternative accommodations, in part because of Airbnb's popularity and the loyalty of the online community that this service has been able to build and maintain.

As a result, Airbnb offers a viable business opportunity for travel hosts around the world. But it's important to understand that Airbnb is not the only short-term rental service hosts can use in order to showcase their property and find travelers willing to pay a nightly, weekly, or monthly fee in order to stay at the property.

Chapter 1 described a handful of other online-based short-term rental services, some of which work very much like Airbnb, while others focus exclusively on renting out entire homes to specific types of travelers. This chapter features interviews with executives from three short-term rental services.

From the following interviews, you'll discover additional strategies for becoming a successful travel host, regardless of which service(s) you use, plus learn more about some of the advantages of using other services, in addition to (or instead of) Airbnb, to list your property.

> **tip**
>
> One of the common traits that many successful travel hosts share is that they simultaneously list their property on multiple short-term rental services. By doing this, they're able to expand the number of people who see their listing, reduce the vacancy rate, and potentially experiment with different nightly rates.

David Adams, CEO of HomeSuite, Discusses How to Become a Successful Travel Host

The HomeSuite service (www.yourhomesuite.com) launched in January 2015, and offers a way for house, condo, or apartment owners to tap into the short-term rental business as a way to generate income by offering their entire property to guests. What sets this service apart, however, is that HomeSuite requires a 30-day minimum stay, but tenants can book a property for up to one full year via a month-to-month lease.

As of late 2016, HomeSuite's service included more than 15,000 property listings within San Francisco, Los Angeles, New York City, Seattle, Boston, Chicago, and Washington, DC. "We are actively working to expand the service into other major U.S. cities in 2017 and beyond," says Adams. "We are currently accepting listings from property owners in other U.S. markets as well."

HomeSuite employs licensed brokers and carefully vets each and every property, landlord, and tenant to ensure that all parties benefit and that expectations are met. "HomeSuite is a marketplace for monthly furnished rentals. Think of it as kind of like Airbnb, but we only do monthly rentals, so all guests sign a short-term lease. The property owners we work with are looking for steadier revenue but want to earn a higher rent rate than they'd otherwise receive offering the same property as a long-term [annual] rental," explains Adams.

▶ Keep Your Availability Calendars Up to Date

If you opt to list your property simultaneously with multiple services, it's important that you manually update the availability calendar on each service, every time you receive a new confirmed booking. Otherwise, if you accidently double-book the same property and wind up needing to cancel one of the confirmed reservations, you'll be penalized by the short-term rental service and earn negative reviews.

Several independent short-term rental property management services offer a single tool that allows the same property listing to be updated simultaneously on multiple services. In addition to an optional service, called Pillow (www.pillowhomes.com), several others are listed in the "Airbnb Property Management Tools and Services" section in the Appendix.

As of late 2016, Pillow operates in San Francisco (and surrounding areas), Los Angeles (and surrounding areas), San Diego, and Seattle, with additional cities (and their surrounding areas) being added on a regular basis.

When a property owner signs up with Pillow, they work with a "Pillow Pro" to ensure that the property is indeed ready to rent. The service then creates a detailed and well-written property listing on the property owner's behalf, does research to set (and when necessary update) the best possible nightly rate, and simultaneously adds the property listing to Airbnb, HomeAway, VRBO, and other comparable online services.

Pillow then handles the reservations, guest check-in process (including the key exchanges), provides 24/7 guest support, and coordinates professional cleaning services for the property. Pillow only works with property owners looking to use short-term rentals to rent their entire home, apartment, or condo.

In most situations, Pillow charges a commission equal to 15 percent of the rental income it helps to generate. This is in addition to the hosting fees charged by the actual short-term rental service each guest booking is done through. For example, Airbnb charges a 3 percent host service fee. Thus, in exchange for being able to turn over most property management responsibility, property owners pay a total fee of 18 percent if a booking is done through Airbnb via Pillow.

Pillow offers a separate "fixed income guarantee" to property owners that meet certain criteria in terms of property type and availability.

"When a host works with Airbnb, they can typically expect a fairly high vacancy rate. For example, a 50 percent vacancy rate is rather common. However, when a guest stays for a whole month or longer, the property owner earns consistent revenue for that entire period. The nightly rate will be lower than what they'd earn for shorter-term rentals through a service like Airbnb, but higher than if they had a tenant sign a one-year lease," adds Adams. "Our property owners generate more revenue over the long term than if they worked with a service like Airbnb, and they have a greater ability to accurately forecast future revenue."

Thanks to its 30-day-minimum-stay requirement, HomeSuite attracts a different clientele than Airbnb when it comes to guests or tenants. He adds, "The people who take advantage of our short-term rental offerings are typically not leisure travelers. We generally attract business professionals [who] are relocating, or who are on a temporary work assignment, and . . . looking for a place to stay that's more homelike and comfortable than a hotel."

The concept for HomeSuite came about as a result of Adams's experience as a tenant. "For my entire adult life, I have only lived in monthly furnished housing. I moved around a lot, and when I was in a city for a longer period, I never knew when I would be moving, so I always stuck with a month-to-month rental of a furnished apartment. This gave me flexibility to be able to move with short notice, when it became necessary," says Adams. "What HomeSuite offers is housing that's on-demand and flexible, and that's designed to fit someone's mobile lifestyle."

The majority of property owners that work with HomeSuite are investors who want to make money from the real estate that they own. They are property owners who buy and retain real estate, and then earn a much higher rental rate through HomeSuite than they would if they offered the same property to tenants through an annual lease. "There is a higher guest turnover rate with tenants using a monthly rental business plan, versus an annual rental business plan, but it's much easier and more cost effective for the property owner than offering their property as a nightly rental that by default has a very high guest turnover rate," says Adams.

Instead of having to deal with the nightly turnover of guests, a property owner who uses HomeSuite can move a guest in for one or more months and then move on to managing their other properties, or pursue their full-time job, and easily manage the properties rented through HomeSuite with much less of an ongoing time commitment. "We work with many property owners who start with just one extra house or property, but find that this is such a lucrative opportunity, that they wind up acquiring additional properties," explains Adams.

It's important to understand that HomeSuite will not accept just any house, apartment, or condo into its offerings. Adams adds, "The property must be fully furnished and include everything that's needed to live there. The guest should be able to arrive with just their suitcase. We also do not accept sublets, and the property owner must be willing to have a tenant for between 30 days and one year. Our tenants are looking for unique places to stay, but they're also looking for a great price, as well as a degree of standardization."

In terms of property standardization, HomeSuite requires a few key things that it knows its tenants are looking for. This includes wifi internet access, parking, a washer and dryer, and a full kitchen. "The core of the HomeSuite service for our property owners is 'less hassle and more profit.' In our view, we offer a more profitable option than long-term rentals or nightly rentals. The way our booking works is very streamlined. There is no back and forth communication or price negotiations between the landlord and tenant. Our reservation system offers the same type of experience as if a guest is booking a hotel room," explains Adams.

"The property owners do not have to field a lot of inquiries from prospective tenants. Instead, they get one notification once they have a confirmed booking through HomeSuite. Our entire marketplace works very much like Airbnb's Instant Book service, but for a complete home, apartment, or condo. The experience is very easy for the property owner and the tenant. HomeSuite also offers a series of guarantees to property owners related to the tenants.

"We guarantee against property damage and require a security deposit from tenants, which protects our landlords. We also have a guarantee beyond that for any incremental damage. And we guarantee that tenants will pay their rent for the period they reserve the property for, for an amount up to $50,000. Our customer care department is able to handle most of the problems or questions that a tenant might have, which puts less of a burden on the landlord," says Adams. "Unlike Airbnb, we perform credit and criminal background checks on every tenant, and we also run title and criminal background checks on our landlords. Both sides are vetted to ensure a very low rate of fraudulent activity."

Because HomeSuite focuses on a booking model, the service heavily emphasizes its review system and allows landlords and tenants alike to publish detailed reviews about each other at the conclusion of a lease. Within a review, a tenant can include actual photos or video clips of the unit they rented, in order to provide a truly accurate representation of the property. "These tenant photos allow future guests to see what the unit will look like day to day when they're living there and are shown in addition to the professionally taken property images that the landlord supplies with their listing," says Adams.

In terms of nightly prices that the tenants wind up paying, HomeSuite's rates tend to be around 40 percent lower than nightly rentals, and 30 to 50 percent higher per night than what someone would pay for an annual rental. He adds, "Keep in mind, it's very common for a nightly rental property, through Airbnb, to have a 50 percent vacancy rate, for example. For people who rent monthly through us, their overall vacancy rate is closer to 15 percent. As a result, if you look at revenue earned at the end of a full year, the total revenue for the property owner that works with HomeSuite is much higher than working with a nightly or annual renting service."

HomeSuite works with each of its landlords to help ensure their success. This includes personalized assistance when it comes to setting competitive nightly rates and creating an attention-getting listing. "We put a strong emphasis on showcasing great property photos and including a well-written and detailed property description. We also encourage the landlords to keep us abreast of the property's availability status. When this information is presented to tenants in conjunction with favorable reviews, this really helps the landlord improve their occupancy rate with good tenants," says Adams.

According to Adams, from the time a property owner first makes contact with HomeSuite, it typically takes just a few weeks to get a property properly listed on the site and for bookings to start coming in. "This depends a lot on our property owners, and how quickly they provide us with the information and photos that are required for the listing. Once a property is listed on HomeSuite, our goal is to provide a seamless booking experience. Our overall focus is on generating more profit with less hassle for the property owners," adds Adams.

Laura Hall, an Executive with Kid & Coe, Explains How Families Are Using Short-Term Rentals

Based in the United Kingdom, Kid & Coe (www.kidandcoe.com) refers to itself as a "family travel platform" that offers entire, multi-bedroom family homes on a short-term rental basis. The service represents homes and properties throughout the world, with its strongest market being the United States.

Unlike Airbnb, this service is fully curated, in that each property is carefully selected by Kid & Coe representatives, which ensures that its offerings meet the family-friendly standards that its renters from around the world are looking for. The company currently represents more than 1,000 properties around the world, with new listings being added daily.

"The main difference between Airbnb and Kid & Coe is that we attract a very select niche of clients, which comprises upscale families that travel. We represent properties with multiple bedrooms, including bedrooms suitable for children, and that have other amenities that families will appreciate. We represent properties that are located in or near family-friendly vacation destinations. For us, however, 'family' is a very broad term. The goal of this service is to help property owners make money through short-term rentals, while providing families with appropriate and comfortable accommodations when they travel," explains Hall.

In addition to furnished homes, Kid & Coe also accepts listings for cabins and other types of accommodations that are suitable for families. "Our property owners include people renting out their second home, vacation home, or their investment properties, as well as people who travel for several weeks during the year and want to generate revenue from their primary home while they're away," says Hall.

Any homeowner can submit their property to be listed on the Kid & Coe service. The process is rather straightforward. The property owner is encouraged to provide all of the requested property details and photos.

The Kid & Coe team then evaluates the listing to determine its suitability for the service, based on how family-friendly it is and what appeal it will have for an upscale traveling family. "We also consider the property's location. There are some areas in any country that you would not want to take your kids to during a vacation. The property may be suitable for a young couple that's looking to enjoy the local nightlife, but not for a family traveling with kids or teens," says Hall.

Based on its selection criteria, Hall reports that only about one-third of the submitted properties get approved for the Kid & Coe service. "If you own a property that you think you want to list with Kid & Coe, I recommend you browse through our service, examine a handful of the existing property listings, and then see for yourself if your property is comparable.

"Understand that part of the property-listing-submission process includes the property owner needing to complete a questionnaire, which should take about 20 minutes. They're asked questions like, 'Why is the property suitable for adults?' and 'What makes it suitable for kids?' You'll be asked to identify any hazards, for example, that would prevent the property from being suitable for young children, as opposed to teenagers," she adds. "We also ask the property owner to submit a lot of photos and to take their time completing the application so we get a really good idea about what's being offered."

Because each property submission is carefully evaluated by a member of the Kid & Coe staff and then the company creates the detailed property listing, the process takes approximately eight weeks between the initial questionnaire submission and when the accepted property actually gets a published listing. "We look at and verify all of the information that's provided by the property owner and then compile additional information that's needed for the listing. Our listing process is much more in depth than the process for listing a property with Airbnb, for example," says Hall. "The benefit is that you'll ultimately be attracting an upscale family to stay at your property, who will be willing to pay a premium nightly rate."

Kid & Coe has an established list of policies and regulations that all guests must adhere to, and a security deposit is collected from all guests. Once a potential guest family expresses interest in a property, they're put in touch with the property owner, who can then collect any additional information they desire about the family, before the booking is accepted. According to Hall, the average booking by a traveling family is between five and seven nights, and most property owners have a four- or five-night minimum stay associated with their listing.

Although recommendations are offered by Kid & Coe, it's up to each property owner to set their nightly rate for guests. "If a family were to book hotel accommodations, they'd typically require two hotel rooms to accommodate everyone. We try to keep our pricing in the same range as booking two hotel rooms in the same area where each property is located," explains Hall. "There is a vast range of prices on our site, however. We have properties that go for up to $20,000 per night, and some priced less than $100.00 per night."

Kid & Coe charges between a 10 and 12 percent commission to its property owners for each booking and handles all aspects of the reservation process, including all financial transactions with the guests. "At first, a property owner might not make a lot of money, because there may be costs involved with getting property prepared to host guests. For example, they'll need to buy new bedding linens and towels. However, over time, this is a viable money-making opportunity," says Hall.

"What we have found is that the biggest concern from property owners who are thinking about using short-term rentals as a way to generate income is a fear of being robbed. Because we're targeting an affluent, family-oriented client base, this has never been an issue for our property owners.

"The biggest challenge that most property owners have is developing and maintaining the right level of communication between themselves and their guests. Property owners have to communicate clearly and honestly when describing their space and when explaining to a guest what's acceptable within their home, for example. Guests need to be told where things are located, how to operate things within the home, and how to acquire the key upon their arrival. The main complaints we receive from guests is that the host has not properly communicated with them or provided necessary information in a clear and easy to understand way," adds Hall.

Just like when using Airbnb, all guests and hosts who opt to use Kid & Coe's service need to create a personal profile that describes them and their family. Then, once a potential guest finds a property where he or she wants to stay, a booking request is submitted to the host. The host can then communicate with the prospective guest and either accept or reject the booking request. Once a booking has been confirmed, the host and guest are free to communicate as much as is necessary either through the service, using email, or by telephone. "Some guests ask lots of questions and require a lot of the host's time prior to check in. Others require much more minimal communication," says Hall. "The key to being a good host when using any short-term rental service is maintaining good communication with your guests."

One new feature being introduced on the Kid & Coe service in 2017 is called Kid & Coe Exchange, which allows any property owner with a listing on the Kid & Coe site to do a house swap with any other property owner who also has a current listing on the site. "As well as renting out your house by the night, a family can do a house swap and pay less than $150.00 per year to participate in this service," adds Hall.

Steffen Bruenn, CEO of Yachtico, Talks About How Boat Owners Can Benefit from Short-Term Rentals

Airbnb, and other services like it, all offer a selection of unusual, one-of-a-kind, or extremely high-end accommodation options that are offered as a nightly short-term rental. Historic castles, oceanfront bungalows, and luxury penthouse suites in major cities are among these specialized offerings. While it's possible to also list your yacht as a short-term rental via Airbnb, this is certainly not what the site is best known for. It is, however, what Yachtico (www.yachtico.com) specializes in.

Currently, the Yachtico service has listings for more than 16,000 yachts located around the world. The size of each yacht is between 24 and 70 feet long. Some of the boats are associated with a charter company, and come with a captain, skipper, and/or crew as part of the rental fee.

"We have developed a booking platform where the yacht owner or charter company creates a listing on our website, and then they go through a ten-step due diligence process on our end. They're also asked to supply detailed photographs of their vessel.

"A user can then visit the Yachtico website, enter where and when they want to rent a boat, and see all of the applicable yacht listings that are available. We offer a lot of bare boat charters, as well as yachts that come with a captain or skipper," says Bruenn. "The booking process is very much like booking a hotel room and requires an upfront credit card payment, as well as a damage deposit that's typically equal to the one-week charter price."

Once a reservation is completed, the renter can fly to the location where the yacht is located and, for an additional fee, be picked up at the airport and be brought to the marina where the yacht is docked and waiting to be picked up. The check-in procedure is done at the marina.

A boat owner looking to rent a vessel through Yachtico should visit the company's website (www.yachtico.com/offer-a-boat) and complete the questionnaire. The company charges a commission rate of between 13 and 19 percent per booking.

All boats that are chartered (rented) through the Yachtico platform are fully insured by the boat owner, who must acquire special charter insurance above and beyond the personal insurance they maintain on the vessel that covers their own usage of it. In some countries or regions, the boat also needs to be registered as a charter yacht, as opposed to a private-use vessel.

"We are looking for yachts that meet certain quality-level criteria. If the boat qualifies to be listed with Yachtico, we connect the boat owner with a participating local marina or charter company that we already work with. We need to ensure the boat is well maintained, kept clean, and that the renters will be greeted by customer-service-oriented professionals when they pick up their boat," says Bruenn.

"Out of all of the yacht owners that apply to have their vessel listed on the Yachtico service, almost 95 percent of them are rejected. If a boat has not been properly maintained, or does not offer the proper safety gear, for example, we won't accept a listing for it, because that reflects badly on Yachtico," he adds.

One thing that Yachtico has discovered, which also applies to the short-term rental of traditional properties, is that a yacht (or property) listing with plenty of really good-quality photos will rent out ten times more often than a similar offering that is not showcased as well or as thoroughly using photos.

"We provide a free ten-page photo guide that explains how to take professional-quality photos of your own vessel. However, we also recommend that a professional photographer be hired to take the required photos, since images play such a vital role in the rental process.

"It's also essential that the text description really emphasizes what makes the yacht special or unique. This would also apply to a property listing. We have found that the accuracy of the listing is very important, since this is one of the key factors that help to set the renter's expectations. If the description is overhyped, what's being offered will not live up to the expectations that are created, and the renter will ultimately be disappointed," adds Bruenn.

There are many online services that offer peer-to-peer, short-term rentals for yachts. What sets Yachtico apart from these services is the emphasis it places on listing only vessels that are well maintained, clean, and safe for the renter.

"Currently, Yachtico is particularly active in three primary markets, which are the Mediterranean, Caribbean, and Asia. Over the next few years, we see ourselves becoming the premiere yacht rental and charter service in these markets," says Bruenn.

Travel Hosting Resources

They say you can never be rich enough or young enough. While these points could be argued, we believe you can never have enough resources. Therefore, we present a wealth of sources for you to check into, check out, and harness for your own personal information blitz.

These sources are tidbits, ideas to get you started on your research. They are by no means the only sources out there, and they should not be taken as the Ultimate Answer. We have done our research, but businesses do tend to move, change, fold, and expand. As we have repeatedly stressed, do your homework. Get out and start investigating.

Directory of Resources

Throughout this book, you have been provided with a curated selection of resources that can be helpful to prepare you to become a travel host. The following is a summary of these resources, along with a few additional ones, sorted by category.

Short-Term Rental Services

The following are the short-term rental services mentioned throughout this book. Keep in mind, some of these require hosts to rent their entire house or apartment, as opposed to one or more bedrooms within a property.

- ▶ *Airbnb.* www.airbnb.com
- ▶ *FlipKey.* www.flipkey.com
- ▶ *HomeAway.* www.homeaway.com
- ▶ *HomeSuite.* www.yourhomesuite.com
- ▶ *Kid & Coe.* www.kidandcoe.com
- ▶ *OneFineStay.* www.onefinestay.com
- ▶ *Roomorama.* www.roomorama.com
- ▶ *Travelmob.* www.travelmob.com
- ▶ *TripAdvisor Short-Term Rentals.* https://rentals.tripadvisor.com/register
- ▶ *Tripping.* www.tripping.com
- ▶ *Vacation Rentals.* www.vacationrentals.com
- ▶ *VRBO.* www.vrbo.com
- ▶ *Yachtico.* www.yachtico.com (this pertains only to boats)

Airbnb Web Pages and Contact Phone Numbers

The following Airbnb phone numbers and URLs provide up-to-date information about specific information pertinent to hosts. Because Airbnb's policies and guidelines are periodically updated, it's essential that as a host, you stay up to date on these changes.

- ▶ *Airbnb Customer Service Phone Numbers.* (855) 424-7262 or (415) 800-5959
- ▶ *Airbnb for Business Host Information.* www.airbnb.com/business-travel-ready, and www.airbnb.com/help/article/1185/what-makes-a-listing-business-travel-ready
- ▶ *Airbnb Open Events Information.* https://airbnbopen.com
- ▶ *Airbnb Referral Program Information.* www.airbnb.com/referrals/terms_and_conditions
- ▶ *Badge Information.* www.airbnb.com/users/badges
- ▶ *Contact Airbnb.* www.airbnb.com/help/contact_us

▶ *Content Policy.* www.airbnb.com/help/article/546/what-is-airbnb-s-content-policy

▶ *Extortion Policy.* www.airbnb.com/help/article/548/what-is-airbnb-s-extortion-policy

▶ *Host Cancelation Penalty Information.* www.airbnb.com/help/article/990/i-m-a-host--what-penalties-apply-if-i-need-to-cancel-a-reservation

▶ *Host Guarantee Information.* www.airbnb.com/guarantee

▶ *Host Protection Insurance Information.* www.airbnb.com/host-protection-insurance

▶ *Listing of all Airbnb Terms and Policies.* www.airbnb.com/help/topic/250/terms--policies

▶ *Payout Policies.* www.airbnb.com/help/article/459/how-do-i-calculate-my-payout

▶ *Property Photographer Information.* www.airbnb.com/info/photography

▶ *Resolution Center.* www.airbnb.com/resolutions

▶ *Review Guidelines.* www.airbnb.com/help/article/13/how-do-reviews-work

▶ *Security Deposit Information.* www.airbnb.com/help/article/352/what-happens-if-a-host-makes-a-claim-on-my-security-deposit

▶ *Standards & Expectations Policies.* www.airbnb.com/standards

▶ *Superhost Information.* www.airbnb.com/superhost

▶ *Tax-Related Information.* www.airbnb.com/help/article/481/how-do-taxes-work-for-hosts

Airbnb's Social Media Links

Engage with Airbnb employees and fellow hosts via Airbnb's social media presence.

▶ *Facebook.* www.facebook.com/airbnb

▶ *Instagram.* www.instagram.com/airbnb

▶ *Twitter.* www.twitter.com/Airbnb or www.twitter.com/AirbnbHelp

▶ *YouTube.* www.youtube.com/user/Airbnb

▶ *Google+.* https://plus.google.com/+Airbnb

▶ *LinkedIn.* www.linkedin.com/company/Airbnb

▶ *Airbnb Community Center.* https://community.airbnb.com/t5/Community-Center/ct-p/community-center

▶ *Airbnb Meetup Information.* www.airbnb.com/meetups

Airbnb Property Management Tools and Services

If you can't be available to greet your guests, oversee cleanup in between guests, or manage your bookings, there are a growing number of independent companies that can assist you with these and other hosting responsibilities (for a fee, of course).

- ▶ *Airbnb Host Help.* www.airbnb.com/help
- ▶ *AirbnbEazy (UK-Based).* http://airbnbeazy.com
- ▶ *GuestReady (UK-Based).* www.guestready.com/en-uk/london
- ▶ *Guesty Host Management Service.* www.guesty.com
- ▶ *Host'n Up.* www.hostnup.com
- ▶ *HostTonight.* www.hosttonight.com
- ▶ *Properly.* www.getproperly.com
- ▶ *Urban Bellhop.* http://urbanbellhop.com

Additional Airbnb Host Resources

The following resources include independently operated and information-packed blogs, as well as additional third-party tools and services available to travel hosts.

- ▶ *Abundant Host.* Blog—http://theabundanthost.com/resources
- ▶ *Airbnb Host Forum.* An independent online community for Airbnb hosts—www.airhostsforum.com
- ▶ *Angie's List.* Find recommended, licensed, and insured home repair experts in your area, including electricians, plumbers, heating/AC specialist, contractors, painters, and house cleaning services—www.angieslist.com
- ▶ *HomeAdvisor.* Find recommended, licensed, and insured home repair experts in your area, including electricians, plumbers, heating/AC specialist, contractors, painters, and house cleaning services—www.homeadvisor.com
- ▶ *Hurdlr.* Travel host tax and bookkeeping information—https://hurdlr.com/blog/airbnb-host
- ▶ *Payoneer Prepaid Debit MasterCard.* www.payoneer.com/prepaid-mastercard
- ▶ *PayPal.* www.paypal.com
- ▶ *Pillow.* List and manage your short-term rental property across multiple services simultaneously—www.pillowhomes.com
- ▶ *QuickBooks Accounting/Bookkeeping Software.* https://quickbooks.intuit.com
- ▶ *Ryze.* Home manual creation tool—http://tryryze.com/info
- ▶ *Welcome Letter Template from Airbnb Guide.* www.airbnbguide.com/sample-airbnb-guest-welcome-sheet-download/
- ▶ *Your Welcome.* Specialized tablet for Airbnb hosts—www.yourwelcome.com

Furniture, Décor, and Property Enhancement Resources

When it comes to furnishing, decorating, and keeping your property stocked with the items that are needed, the following businesses and services can help you save money and handle some of your shopping needs online.

- ▶ *Amazon Prime.* www.amazon.com/prime
- ▶ *Ashley Home Store.* www.ashleyfurniturehomestore.com
- ▶ *Bed, Bath & Beyond.* www.bedbathandbeyond.com
- ▶ *BJ's Wholesale Club.* www.bjs.com
- ▶ *CB2.* www.cb2.com
- ▶ *Costco.* www.costco.com
- ▶ *Crate & Barrel.* www.crateandbarrel.com
- ▶ *Furniture Warehouse.* www.thefurniturewarehouse.net
- ▶ *Grandin Road.* www.grandinroad.com
- ▶ *Home Decorators Collection.* www.homedecorators.com
- ▶ *Ikea.* www.ikea.com
- ▶ *Overstock.* www.overstock.com
- ▶ *Pier 1.* www.pier1.com
- ▶ *Pottery Barn.* www.potterybarn.com
- ▶ *Wayfair.* www.wayfair.com

Mobile App-Based Food and Item Delivery Services

Once you determine which food delivery services work in your geographic area, consider offering information about them within your home manual, as a resource for your guests.

To find additional mobile apps focused on restaurant and food delivery services, visit the App Store (iPhone/iPad) or Google Play Store (Android), and within the search field, enter the phrase, "food delivery" or "restaurant delivery."

- ▶ *Amazon Prime Now.* http://primenow.amazon.com
- ▶ *Grubhub.* www.grubhub.com
- ▶ *UberEATS.* https://ubereats.com
- ▶ *Yelp Eat24.* https://eat24hours.com

Nationwide Maid/House Cleaning Services

In addition to the many independently operated maid or home cleaning services that are likely offered in your geographic area (check your Yellow Pages or do an online search), the following is information about national referral services, as well as cleaning services with local franchises across the United States.

- ▶ *Care.com.* www.care.com/housekeepers
- ▶ *HomeAdvisor.* www.homeadvisor.com/category.Cleaning-Maid-Services.12014.html
- ▶ *Local Cleaning Pros.* www.localcleaningpros.com
- ▶ *Merry Maids.* www.merrymaids.com
- ▶ *Molly Maid.* www.mollymaid.com

Nightly Price Setting Tools

As a host, setting your nightly rate can be a challenge. There are multiple factors to consider, and relevant information you'll need (such as local demand) changes daily. To help you set and continuously update your nightly pricing, and potentially increase your revenue as a travel host by between 10 and 40 percent, consider using one of the following online tools or services. All work with Airbnb, and some work with other popular short-term rental services as well.

- ▶ *Beyond Pricing.* https://beyondpricing.com
- ▶ *Brite Yield.* http://briteyield.com
- ▶ *Everbooked.* www.everbooked.com
- ▶ *PriceLabs.* www.pricelabs.co (notice this URL does not end with .com)
- ▶ *Smart Host.* http://smarthost.me
- ▶ *Wheelhouse.* www.usewheelhouse.com

Short-Term Rental Insurance

Many home insurance policies do not cover loss, damage, or liability when you offer your property for short-term rental and have paying guests staying in your home. In addition to the insurance provided by Airbnb (or whichever short-term rental service you opt to use), consider acquiring a separate short-term rental insurance policy that protects your property and belongings and that offers the liability coverage you'll need.

- ▶ *Comet Insurance.* www.comethome.com
- ▶ *P Fudge & Associates, Inc.* https://fudgeinsurance.com/short-term-rental-insurance
- ▶ *Proper Insurance.* www.proper.insure

Smart Locks (Keyless-Entry Door Locks)

Instead of using traditional key-based locks on their doors, many travel hosts utilize more cutting-edge smart locks, which provide a programmable and customizable keyless-entry solution for your guests. The following is information about a handful of smart lock companies.

▶ *Home Depot.* www.homedepot.com/s/smartlocks
▶ *Kwikset.* www.kwikset.com/SmartSecurity/Re-Key-Technology.aspx
▶ *Lowe's.* www.lowes.com/search?searchTerm=smart+locks
▶ *RemoteLock.* http://remotelock.com/Airbnb
▶ *Keycafe.* www.keycafe.com
▶ *Lockitron.* https://lockitron.com

Glossary

Advance Notice: This is the amount of time you need as a host, between the time a guest makes a reservation and when he or she checks in.

Airbnb Business Travel Ready: Airbnb hosts can cater to business travelers and potentially charge a premium nightly rate but must adhere to providing a predetermined set of amenities set by Airbnb and cater specifically to the unique needs of business travelers.

Airbnb Instant Book: Airbnb hosts can turn on this feature to allow guests to book and confirm their reservation, without first being approved by hosts.

Airbnb Open: These are fee-based, organized gatherings of Airbnb hosts that provide workshops, speakers, and networking opportunities that can teach hosts how to improve their travel hosting business.

Airbnb Resolution Center: The online tools offered by Airbnb that are available to guests and hosts, used to resolve disagreements, report complaints, mediate problems, and settle financial disputes.

Airbnb Secure Messaging System: The centralized messaging service used by Airbnb guests and hosts to communicate prior to the in-person check-in process. Messages can be sent and received via the Airbnb website or mobile app. Personal information about the host or guest is not provided via this service, so a level of anonymity and security is offered until a reservation is made and confirmed.

Airbnb Smart Pricing: An automated tool that allows hosts to auto-adjust their nightly rate, based on localized demand and other factors.

Airbnb Superhost: These are experienced and highly rated Airbnb hosts who have met or exceeded Airbnb's strict guidelines to earn this designation. Many experienced Airbnb guests prefer to stay with Superhosts, because it's an added guarantee that the property will be safe, clean, loaded with amenities, and managed by an experienced and friendly host.

Amenities: The selection of items or services that Airbnb hosts offer to their guests on a complimentary basis. An amenity can be anything from travel-size toiletries to access to a private hot tub.

Bedroom Configuration: Refers to the number of bedrooms, as well as the number of beds, and the size of the beds (twin, queen, king, etc.), within a short-term rental property.

Booking: A reservation made by a guest that gets approved and confirmed by the travel host via a short-term rental service.

Cleaning Fee: In addition to the nighty or weekly rate charged by a host, this is an added fee a host can charge to cover the cost of having the property professionally cleaned after a guest checks out.

Guest: The person who pays a nightly or weekly fee to stay in a guestroom or home that's provided by the travel host.

House Manual: A written document prepared by the host that explains how to use various items in the home, such as the washer, dryer, wifi, or home theater system. It also typically includes the house rules, as well as recommendations for local restaurants and attractions.

House Rules: This is the written set of rules that are compiled by the host, which guests are expected to adhere to. House rules are part of a property listing and should also be provided to guests upon check-in. A no-smoking or no-pets policy are examples of house rules.

Nightly Rate: The fee that a guest pays per night to stay with a travel host, or in a home, apartment, or condo, for example, owned by the host.

Personal Profile: The personal information that a member of the Airbnb community (both hosts and guests) shares online in conjunction with their Airbnb account.

Property: The guestroom, apartment, house, or condo, for example, that the travel host is offering to guests as a short-term rental through a service such as Airbnb.

Property Listing: The information about a property that is being offered by a travel host. This describes details about what's being offered, as well as other information a potential guest needs when deciding where to stay.

Security Deposit: An extra fee, above and beyond the nightly rate, that a guest pays in advance. This fee is used to cover any damage or theft that occurs within the host's property during the guest's stay. If no damage or theft is reported by the host, the security deposit gets refunded shortly after the guest's checkout.

Shared Room: When the guest will be sharing a bedroom, bathroom, or living space with other guests or the host and won't have full privacy. It's common for a private bedroom to have a shared bathroom, or for multiple bedrooms to have a shared kitchen. In fewer cases, a shared bedroom is offered, however.

Short-Term Rental: The term used to describe the process of a travel host providing short-term (less than one month) accommodations to a guest, within their home or the property they own, in exchange for a nightly or weekly fee.

Short-Term Rental Insurance: This is optional insurance that a travel host can acquire that protects the property and belongings against theft and damage, for example, caused by guests. This is separate from the coverage that services like Airbnb offer to its hosts.

Smart Lock Keyless Entry: Instead of using traditional key-based door locks, keyless-entry smart locks allow hosts to share a programmable entry code with guests that can be used to enter the property during a guest's stay.

Travel Host: The person who opens their own home or property to guests in exchange for a nightly or weekly fee.

Vacation Rental Property: This typically refers to an entire home that's offered on a short-term basis to guests for one or more weeks at a time. The host does not stay on the premises.

Verified ID: Using online tools offered by Airbnb and similar services, hosts and guests can have their identification verified by the service. This helps to protect hosts and guests alike. This process involves matching up someone's name with their photo, email address, address, phone number, and government-issued identification.

About the Authors

Jason R. Rich (http://jasonrich.com) is the author of more than 55 books, including several books for Entrepreneur Press that cover small-business topics. These include *Start Your Own Blogging Business, Start Your Own Etsy Business, Design and Launch an Online e-Commerce Business in a Week*, and *The Ultimate Guide to YouTube for Business*.

He's also a frequent contributor to numerous national magazines, major daily newspapers, and popular websites, as well as an accomplished photographer (www.JasonRichPhotography.com). Please follow Jason R. Rich on Twitter (www.twitter.com/jasonrich7) and Instagram (www.instagram.com/jasonrich7).

ENTREPRENEUR MEDIA

For more than 30 years, Entrepreneur Media has been setting the course for small-business success. From startup to retirement, millions of entrepreneurs and small-business owners trust the Entrepreneur Media family—*Entrepreneur* magazine, Entrepreneur.com, Entrepreneur Press, EntrepreneurEnEspanol.com, and our industry partners—to point them in the right direction. The Entrepreneur Media family is regarded as a beacon within the small- to mid-sized business community, providing outstanding content, fresh opportunities, and innovative ways to push publishing, small business, and entrepreneurship forward.

Index